Called to Lead

PRAISE FOR *CALLED TO LEAD*

Called to Lead is a very thorough roadmap—not only for the new leader looking for success, but for seasoned leaders who need to review periodically to "stay out of the ditch." The hands-on techniques that Gwendolyn lays out in supporting the roadmap are invaluable and proven tools for any leader.

—**Donald R. McLaughlin**, Retired, Manager of Business Analysis, International Paper

I had a front-row seat for much of Gwendolyn's leadership journey and had the pleasure of guiding her to discover the leader within. *Called to Lead* is a must-read. In it she shares valuable insights so that new leaders can ramp up the learning curve and become the leader they were meant to be.

—**Bruce J. Patterson**, Retired, Vice President, Internal Audit

Gwendolyn has a proven reputation of success. In *Called to Lead* she shares her experience with other leaders and corporate "Rising Stars" to assist with navigating the sometimes-uncertain pathways of leadership and team development. *Called to Lead* is a "must-read" for leaders at all levels.

—**Ricky L. Tucker**, Founder, RIX International, LLC

Called to Lead addresses the most critical situations leaders will encounter. It's as if two years' worth of education is compiled into one book, which makes for a viable go-to reference. Hands down, this is a must-read for those entering the world of leadership and for veteran leaders!

—**Timothy Florence**, Director of Instructional Services Technology, University of Tennessee

CALLED to LEAD

What to Do When a Leadership Position Finds You

GWENDOLYN J. TUCKER

NEW YORK
LONDON • NASHVILLE • MELBOURNE • VANCOUVER

CALLED to LEAD

What to Do When A Leadership Position Finds You

© 2025 Gwendolyn J. Tucker

All rights reserved. No portion of this book may be reproduced, stored in a retrieval system, or transmitted in any form or by any means—electronic, mechanical, photocopy, recording, scanning, or other—except for brief quotations in critical reviews or articles, without the prior written permission of the publisher.

Published in New York, New York, by Morgan James Publishing. Morgan James is a trademark of Morgan James, LLC. www.MorganJamesPublishing.com

Proudly distributed by Publishers Group West®

A **FREE** ebook edition is available for you or a friend with the purchase of this print book.

CLEARLY SIGN YOUR NAME ABOVE

Instructions to claim your free ebook edition:
1. Visit MorganJamesBOGO.com
2. Sign your name CLEARLY in the space above
3. Complete the form and submit a photo of this entire page
4. You or your friend can download the ebook to your preferred device

ISBN 9781636984278 paperback
ISBN 9781636984285 ebook
Library of Congress Control Number: 2024941123

Cover Design by:
Christopher Kirk
www.GFSstudio.com

Interior Design by:
Chris Treccani
www.3dogcreative.net

Morgan James is a proud partner of Habitat for Humanity Peninsula and Greater Williamsburg. Partners in building since 2006.

Get involved today! Visit: www.morgan-james-publishing.com/giving-back

YOUR GIFT

Cultivate a Great Working Relationship with Your Boss
Your boss is a key link in the chain to your success, both in your current role and your career. Therefore, cultivating a solid working relationship with your boss is to your advantage.

Download this resource to find out
How To Cultivate a Great Working Relationship with Your Boss
Boss Relationship Worksheet

https://bit.ly/boss_relationship_worksheet

DEDICATION

To Mama and Daddy
(my very first leaders)

CONTENTS

Foreword . . . . *xiii*
Introduction . . . . *xv*

Part I: The Four Steps 1

Step 1 - Prepare to Succeed 3
Chapter 1: Your Role and Responsibilities 5
Chapter 2: Your Resources 11
Chapter 3: Your Reporting Hierarchy 15
Chapter 4: Your Organization 17

Step 2—Prepare to Lead 21
Chapter 5: Know Yourself 23
Chapter 6: Know Your Readiness for Your Role 37
Chapter 7: Know Your Relationship with Your Boss 43

Step 3: Prepare the Team 49
Chapter 8: Working Well Together (Team SWOT) 51
Chapter 9: Building High-Performing Teams 53
Chapter 10: Motivating Your Team 63
Chapter 11: Leading in Style 71
Chapter 12: Coaching Your Team Members 79

Step Four: Prepare to Achieve **91**
Chapter 13: Putting It All Together 93

Part II: Leadership Vault **95**

Acknowledgments *153*
About the Author *155*
Appendix I: Resources *157*
Appendix II: Expectations at Work Worksheet *159*
Appendix III: Additional Resources. *163*

FOREWORD

I am in the business of spotting talent. That is what I do. I have been in the recruiting, staffing, and consulting industry for more than forty years, and I have built a very successful career and business doing so. But success didn't just happen in the beginning.

Leadership was something I struggled with in the early years of my company because I'd never seen what GOOD leaders could do and the change they could affect. How I wish I'd had Gwen's counsel a long time ago!

In my business I recruit for major corporations across the United States, some of which are global enterprises. I get to engage with decision makers eager to hire people who possess the skills and competencies needed and who can take the ball and run with it. Time and time again, often in haste, some new leaders are thrown into a leadership position with little to no preparation.

I have known Gwendolyn in a variety of settings, watching as she served as President of NAWBO Memphis, working beside her as a member of the Greater Memphis Chamber's Small Business Council Think Tank, and in professional organizations such as the Society of Entrepreneurs.

It is amazing having the opportunity to observe her gentle leadership and her impeccable character. With such ease, Gwen provides a roadmap to help new leaders as they transition into their first management position. This information and instruction for how to apply it provide the ability to ramp up the learning curve quicker.

There's no limit what you can accomplish by being well prepared to take on the work of leadership.

—**Dotty Summerfield Giusti**
Summerfield Associates, Inc.

INTRODUCTION

I am a leader. I am called upon to do the work of leadership.
—**Michael Gerber**

You've been selected! I've heard that statement more than a time or two during the course of my career.

The first time I heard it was on a day when I was minding my own business, focused on doing my job to the best of my ability. I was presented with the opportunity of a lifetime—I was offered a promotion to become the leader of my team.

The offer came seemingly out of the blue. Quite frankly, I was not lobbying for my boss's position nor had I set my sights on becoming the team leader. I thoroughly enjoyed my job and strived to be a great team player.

In hindsight, I believe that was the very thing that set me up for what later proved to be an amazing opportunity. I was in the right place at the right time and was selected as the right person for the position.

After thinking through the details of the offer, I said yes. Overnight, I was catapulted from being a team member to team leader. I was now the manager of the team with several people reporting to me. Those who used to be my peers were now my direct reports. Talk about a shift in dynamics, literally overnight!

Now, I had received positive feedback on my ability to work well with others, both inside and outside the company. That would actually work in my favor. But I quickly realized that the work of team leader would be very different from the work I was doing as a team member.

At the time of this writing, there are approximately 110 million people employed as full-time workers in the United States of America. Twelve percent of those full-time workers are in some type of leadership position.

If you're reading this and can identify with the 12 percent, that means you are in a leadership position. There's also a very high probability you were an excellent individual contributor who got called to lead—maybe out of the blue, maybe not.

So, what do you do when a leadership position finds you? What do you do after you've said yes to something for which you've had little-to-no preparation and have only an inkling of what you've gotten yourself into?

Some may have to go it alone; thankfully, I had a great boss. His name is Bruce. I had the privilege of working with Bruce for eight years. Under his leadership, I grew both personally and professionally. I am so very grateful to Bruce for bringing out the best in me. He left an indelible imprint in my life and helped me become the leader I am today.

But what if you don't have someone like Bruce to help guide you? The reality for many who are promoted to their first leadership position is that they are thrown into the role without much guidance.

That's why I wrote this book—to help first-time leaders like you ramp up the learning curve, to bring to your attention some things you need to know, and to lay out a roadmap for you to follow as you embark on this new journey called leadership.

The Work of Leadership

As the leader, I was called upon to do the work of leadership. But I had to find out what the work of leadership entailed. What did all this really mean?

I knew how to work. Now, I was charged with getting work done through others. To do that, I had to learn lots about my direct reports. But ultimately, I learned a whole lot more about myself: my strengths, my weaknesses, my adaptability, and where I tended to be inflexible. A former pastor used to say, "Blessed are the flexible for they shall not break." Wise words that helped me in so many ways.

I wish I could say that ramping up the learning curve was easy-breezy. But that would be less than honest and far from reality. The truth is that leading others can be challenging. Learning how to lead yourself can be doubly so.

That's the reason I wrote this book. I want to share some of my successes, yes. But, more than that, I want to share some of my challenges and how I overcame them, in the hopes that you can avoid some of the mistakes I made.

I've heard it said that life is lived forward, but it is understood backward. In this book, I share situations I lived through that I have a better understanding of now, which is what I want to pass on to you for your consideration.

If you have been called to lead and you accepted the call, the information in this book has been written just for you.

This is my story about leadership positions that found me and lessons learned along the way. In it I share insights about leadership theories and how I put them into practice, sometimes clumsily and sometimes getting results I did not want. You will also discover leadership traits and how my experiences helped meld and develop my character. In this book are lessons learned along the way about leading people. One of those people? Me.

There is an age-old debate about whether leaders are born or made. One commentator responded by saying, "Of course leaders are born. Then they are made!" Sometimes the making of a leader doesn't feel good, nor does it look pretty. But I want to share the good, the bad, and the ugly because all were necessary in making me the person I am today. In the pages of this book are words to lead by, written to empower you to become the leader you were born to be. Yes, you've been selected! You are the right person. This is the right position. This is the perfect time to discover the leader in you.

What You Can Expect

I consider it an honor that you would not only buy my book, but also that you would take the time to invest in yourself by reading it. Therefore, here you can expect to find valuable life lessons that I was taught, and some that I caught, along the pathway to becoming the leader I am today.

I have outlined these lessons in a way that makes sense to me, and I believe it will make sense to you as well. Although leadership is both art and science, there is a methodology and framework that can be followed as we develop our leadership skills. The steps are interdependent and are listed in sequence as follows:

>Step One—Prepare to Succeed
>Step Two—Prepare to Lead
>Step Three—Prepare the Team
>Step Four—Prepare to Achieve

All too often we put the cart before the horse. I can attest to that. Perhaps you can too. But for those positions when I got a more complete understanding of what I had signed up for BEFORE I started moving forward, I experienced a greater degree of success.

As you delve into each step, you may have some questions. If so, just jot them down. They may be answered as you read through the book. I include links to additional resources for those who would like to take a deeper dive into the subject. I also include a list of resources in the Appendix.

Plus, I include a summary at the end of each step, along with a checklist you can take and make your own. I realize that each person reading *Call to Lead* will glean different insights that apply to where each individual is right now. Thank you for selecting me to assist you on your leadership journey.

You are in the right place, at the right time.

So, let's begin at the beginning—Step One: Prepare to Succeed!

Part I:
The Four Steps

STEP 1
PREPARE TO SUCCEED

Preparation is key to succeeding in any worthwhile endeavor, especially in leadership.

As a new leader, I want you to get off on the right foot. And the best way to do that is to prepare to succeed. It's quite tempting to dive in headfirst and start working. But first, you must define what "work" means now that you are the leader.

You have been called to a worthwhile endeavor; if you thought otherwise, you would not have accepted the offer. It's imperative that you discover what this worthwhile endeavor entails.

Whether the position is in a for-profit or nonprofit, paid or unpaid, beginning with a clear understanding of what you've said yes to increases your chances of success. Therefore, getting your arms around what you said yes to is a must. Because at the end of the day, this is what you will be held accountable for. So, getting a good understanding of what is expected at the beginning of your assignment is critical to your success. Make sure you find out the details on the following:

- Your Role and Responsibilities
- Your Resources
- Your Reporting Hierarchy
- Your Organization/Company

You may be asking why these are so important. They are important because you have been called to lead in a specific organization. That organization has allotted you certain resources with which you are to get the job done, and these are outlined in your role and responsibilities. You will be reporting to a specific person in the organization who has oversight of you and the area you lead. At the end of the day, or should I say, at the end of each performance period, you will have to give an account of what you've produced with the resources entrusted to you.

I am a big fan of Stephen Covey's *7 Habits of Highly Effective People*. I read it fairly early in my career and, boy, am I glad I did! When you follow what is outlined in Step One—Prepare to Succeed, you will be putting into practice the first habit, "Begin with the end in mind." By doing so, you greatly increase your chances of success in your new position.

A word of caution: You may be tempted to skip Step One, in part or in whole, and move to Step Two. But please, please, please, do not yield to the temptation to do so. Moving to the next step before completing Step One would be like leaving out a key ingredient in your favorite recipe. The outcome? I think you get the picture. Complete this step with gusto. You will thank me later.

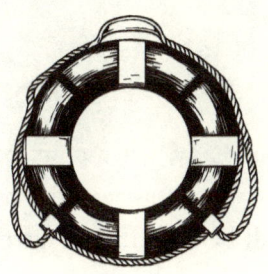

CHAPTER 1
YOUR ROLE AND RESPONSIBILITIES

You may be wondering why I start with urging you to understand your role and responsibilities. If you are moving from team member to a leadership position within the same department or company, it may seem counterintuitive. But it's not. Although you may have read the position description, it's always a good idea to get a comprehensive understanding of what is expected of you in your new position. So yes, please read the position description, but don't stop there. Make sure you have a conversation with your immediate supervisor, whom I lovingly call the boss. Get a clear idea of what is expected—and get it in writing. That way, you will reduce the chances of being surprised at a later date. Plus, being clear on what is expected of you as the leader of a team will help you determine what to communicate to your team in Step Three.

Let's talk about three things you need to know related to roles and responsibilities:
1. Expectations
2. Goals and Objectives
3. KPIs/Metrics

Expectations

If you haven't seen it already, get a copy of the organizational chart for your department. That will show you the positions and names of the people with whom you will be working on a frequent basis.

As a leader, not only do you have expectations of yourself in your new position, but others will have expectations of you as well—your boss, your team, your peers, your company, and your customer (internal and/or external).

Some of these expectations are already written down on paper, but some are unspoken. Those are the ones you need to identify. And the way to do that is to talk to the people who have expectations of you.

It would be a very good idea to have conversations with the following:
1. Your boss
2. Your team members
3. Your peers
4. Your customers (internal and external)

Start by scheduling time with your boss, then with each of your team members. From there, meet with each of your peers. I call them "near peers" since they are part of the team you're on that is headed up by your boss.

The bulk of what is expected will be identified during these discussions; I'd venture to say 80 to 85 percent of what is expected will be ferreted out. But please know that some expectations will only be discovered or revealed as you take on the leadership role for this particular assignment.

I include a more detailed explanation in Chapter 7 about this topic. There's also a checklist in the Appendix to assist you to gain a better understanding of what is expected with conversations.

Goals and Objectives

Identify specific goals and objectives that you and your team will be required to achieve. These goals and objectives align with your organization's goals and objectives outlined in the strategic plan.

If you haven't read the strategic plan yet, please add it to your reading list. As a leader, the company's strategic plan will help you better understand how what you do on a daily basis helps the company meet its goals and objectives.

For instance, as the Customer Relationship Manager for the Food Service Division of a publicly traded company, I was responsible for customer service representatives and financial account specialists for the division. Our customer service representatives played an integral part in keeping customers happy, which meant we were able to retain customers and they were more likely to increase the size of their orders. Plus, our team was a source of intel for the outside sales force, alerting them to a potential problem and nipping problems in the bud before they became unmanageable.

KPIs/Metrics

KPI is an acronym for Key Performance Indicators. Every goal must have a metric attached to it, both quantitative and qualitative. Otherwise, how would you know if the goal was achieved?

For example, for our customer service professionals mentioned above, one of their key performance indicators was OTIFNE. It measured if an order was on time, in full, with no errors. The goal was to achieve a score of 95 percent and was calculated at a minimum on a weekly basis. Getting this information on a weekly basis allowed each representative to make timely adjustments to ensure the goal of 95 percent or better was maintained.

This particular metric—OTIFNE—was very important to our customers. They relied on us to deliver what was needed in a timely manner. Plus, rework can be quite costly, increasing expenses and potentially damaging a company's reputation.

Your job description, if it is well put together, should identify the metrics associated with your position. If not, you should get together with your boss posthaste to clarify how they will assess your performance. For an example of what it means to begin with the end in mind, the process and possible outcome, please see the Appendix.

Using your KPIs, you can build a scorecard that shows your goals and objectives. On it you will record progress made toward reaching your goals. It will also be used when communicating to your team what is expected and how well the team is doing. Reviewing progress against your goals frequently allows you to make adjustments and corrections in a timely manner.

Summary

Getting a clear understanding of what is expected of you in your new leadership position, along with the metrics of how your performance will be evaluated, will help set you up for success.

Not only will you get clarity on what is expected and how it will be measured, but it will make conversations with your direct reports go much easier. I've found that when I'm clear on what is expected, I can better communicate with my team. When all members of the team I lead are very clear on what is expected and on their part in getting the team to success, things go so much smoother.

I go into more detail in Step 3—Prepare Your Team. For now, suffice it to say that when you are clear, communications with your team become crystal clear.

NEXT STEPS

From the information outlined in this Chapter, you have identified what you have or already know that will help you be successful in your leadership role. On the other hand, you may have identified some information you don't have but will need. Create a checklist for yourself to ensure you have all your bases covered. The list should include the following:

- Job Description
- Expectations
- Goals & Objectives
- Metrics
- Department/Team Organizational Chart
- Calendar/Schedule

Add others as needed!

CHAPTER 2
YOUR RESOURCES

As the leader of your team, you will be entrusted with some valuable resources. Money is one, but the most important resource will be the people with whom you work to get the job done. I really like this quote by John C. Maxwell: "A leader knows that people are their most appreciable asset."

So, who are these people? They include:
- The people who report directly to you
- Your fellow team members, also known as your peers
- Your boss or supervisor

If you have met with your direct reports, you have already started to get to know who they are, what they expect, and what they bring to the table. Reviewing their resume or employee record is another way to better understand their past experience, what they do well, and areas where they can improve.

A word of caution when reviewing past performance reviews: Try to remain as objective as possible. You need to know if there is a history of performance problems, but I encourage you to let them prove (or disprove) what they can or cannot do.

If you were promoted within your department, you will already know the folks on your team. Generally speaking, you are familiar with their work, but as the leader, you now have access to information you weren't privy to before. One example of having access to sensitive and confidential data is in the area of payroll. As the leader of the team, you will have access to payroll data for your team. Because you oversee a portion of the budget (more about that later), payroll data will be a large expense item in your budget.

When I was promoted to manager of the team previously composed of my peers, in some cases, making the leap was challenging for me. Some of my peers were close friends, which meant in some cases it was difficult to remain objective. Thankfully, those peers who were also close friends wanted me to succeed and took great care not to put me in an uncomfortable position.

But what if you have been promoted to a leadership position in an area or department where you didn't know your direct reports, your boss, or your peers? In some ways, ignorance really is bliss. You get to start off with a clean slate, and they do too.

Following the steps outlined above, especially meeting with members of your department to understand what is expected and doing your research, is doubly important.

Your Budget

Now to your budget, which represents the financial resources allocated to you and your team. I have a degree in accounting and earned my designation as a Certified Public Accountant after starting my career. My first job out of college was in cost accounting, which laid the foundation for me to understand financial statements, especially the balance sheet and income statement.

Fortunately, you don't have to possess a degree in accounting to understand the basics of your budget, but you do have to learn what the numbers mean. At the end of the day, one of your metrics should be how well you manage the finances entrusted to your care.

Have you seen your budget? If not, ask your boss about it. Some supervisors keep the budget numbers close and are hesitant to share, but at a minimum, you should know which part of the budget you are responsible for and will be held accountable.

Summary

The main point I'd like you to take away from this chapter is that you have resources at your disposal—or resources you have been given to get the job done and get it done well. Become familiar with your resources and how you will be held accountable for using them.

Always remember that the most valuable of all the resources you have to work with are your people. They are your most important asset. Treat them as prized possessions, and you will be amazed at what you and your team can accomplish.

NEXT STEPS
- Collect your thoughts and summarize your notes from this Chapter.
- Make sure you are well acquainted with the resources at your disposal. Use them well.
- If you have not reviewed the budget for your team and discussed the numbers with your boss, please do so posthaste. Get a clear understanding from your boss of what is required, as well as how often you two will review it together. By reviewing your budget each month and each quarter, you will know if you are within or over your budget. If expenses are over budget, you can take measures to rein in spending.

CHAPTER 3

YOUR REPORTING HIERARCHY

You may wonder why I have included this little chapter, but knowing your reporting hierarchy gives you a line of sight on the progression within your department. This is your field of dreams. It shows you what could be next as it relates to moving up within your organization.

Yes, you are new to your role, but you need to know what the hierarchy looks like for your department and the organization. Depending upon your company, it should be easy to access the org chart. It was probably covered in your onboarding. If not, talk with your immediate supervisor. They will have one or know where to get one.

Of course, your immediate supervisor is the person with whom you work most often and will get to know the best. But you also need to know the name (and face) of your boss's boss. I say that because your boss's boss is a key decision maker in all things related to you. They approve your hiring, your performance rating, your annual raise, and so on.

In the companies where I've worked, I knew who was in charge as least three levels up. Not only did I know them—they knew me too.

Summary

Know who is on your team. We spend a lot of time at work. Many of us spend more time with our colleagues at work than we do with some of our family members. It's only natural that we get to know each other.

NEXT STEPS

Get a copy of your company's organization chart. If you are new to the department or company, make it a point to meet at least one new person at work each week.

I'm amazed at the number of people I've met at work. In some cases, we started out being co-workers, then professional friends, and finally friends outside work. I still keep in touch with colleagues I worked with many, many years ago. Perhaps you will too.

CHAPTER 4
YOUR ORGANIZATION

Your organization or employer is what brings you and your co-workers together. Your workplace is the common denominator.

The mission, vision, and core values bind you together and point to what unites you. It's where you find common ground. It's your reason for being, your raison d'être. Since it's the reason your job exists, it's imperative that you become acquainted with your company's:
- Mission
- Vision
- Core Values

The vision represents why the company exists. The mission expresses what the company must do every day to achieve the vision. And the core values represent by what standard or code of conduct employees are to achieve the mission and vision.

Vision statements tend to be quite lofty and seemingly unattainable, especially in the short-term. But the vision represents something to strive toward to make the world a better place.

My husband and I reside in the Memphis area. St. Jude Children's Research Hospital is an icon, not only in Memphis but around the world. Just to hear the story of how it all got started is amazing in and of itself. Founded by Danny Thomas, St. Jude opened in 1982 with the dream that "no child should die in the dawn of life." Out of that dream was born the vision that "no child is denied treatment based on race, religion, or a family's ability to pay." The mission, what the hospital is charged with doing every single day, is to "advance cures and means of prevention for pediatric catastrophic diseases through research and treatment."

Now, your company may not be in the business of saving the lives of children, but for your company to survive and thrive, you have to solve a problem that a customer is willing to pay for. Your position exists because it is a needed link in the supply chain for solving your customer's problems. So, being well acquainted with the vision, mission, and core values of your company is very important, especially if you are a leader.

As a leader, you represent your company. If you don't know the vision, mission, and core values, how can you relay them to your team and model them in the way you lead? It is impossible to be and do something you do not know.

Core values set the standard by which you do what you do each day. Often, core values for a company will include something related to service, integrity, safety, and team play.

Do you know your company's vision, mission and core values? Could you recite them from memory? If not, I encourage you to add it to your list and take action. The beautiful thing about this step is that, once you learn it, you won't have to do it again because they don't change often.

Summary

By this point you may feel like you're drinking water through a firehose—which is impossible to do, by the way. But don't despair, there is a way to pace yourself. Rome wasn't built in a day.

Grab a copy of your company's vision, mission, and core values. Put them in a conspicuous place where you can see them often and be reminded of why you're at your place of work and the things that bind you and your fellow associates together. This is what you work toward and invest valuable resources in achieving on a daily basis.

If you're feeling overwhelmed by all you have to do, I have a resource you will find helpful. I'm pretty confident of this fact, because I use it and have recommended it to many who are in their first leadership position. *The First 90 Days* by Michael D. Watkins is a book I highly recommend. Even if you don't read the entire book, please check out the summary.

Once you become familiar with what he calls critical success strategies for new leaders, you will find it helpful in ramping up the learning curve as you progress in your career.

NEXT STEPS

Get a copy of the following:
- Mission Statement
- Vision Statement
- Core Values

To go the extra mile and really stand out from the crowd, commit them to memory. That way, they will roll off your tongue effortlessly.

If you are going to be an effective leader, you must be prepared.
—Dr. Myles Monroe

STEP 2—PREPARE TO LEAD

As you prepare to lead, it will be important to know yourself better, gauge your readiness for this new leadership position, and cultivate a great working relationship with your boss.

You may be thinking you already know yourself pretty well. I am sure you do as it relates to what was required of you in your prior jobs. But this is different. As a leader, you will be called upon to do the work of leadership, which means you must assess your readiness to step up to what will be demanded in your new position.

CHAPTER 5
KNOW YOURSELF

Now that you have been promoted to a leadership position, one of the best things you can do is listen, listen, listen. You will be listening for information that will prove valuable as you ramp up the learning curve. Some of the information you will use now, some later, and some never.

By all means, listen to your boss. Your boss will have a wealth of knowledge about your position, your direct reports, and the team or department you are leading.

Listen to your direct reports. Listen to your peers. Listen to your customers, regardless of whether they are internal, external, or both.

This may seem odd, but one of the most important persons to listen to is *you*. Pay attention to questions that arise, thoughts about your new role, and the path you think you should take. Even listen to any doubts that may arise. Not that you will give in to them, but they will alert you to areas of concern in which you can be proactive and silence the doubts.

In knowing yourself, it's important that we discuss leadership and styles. You may think I'm referring to leadership styles such as autocratic, participative, or laissez-faire. No, not yet. I go into more detail about those later.

Here, I mean those "styles" that directly affect a leader's ability to get work done through others, such as:

- Personality
- Learning
- Communication
- Conflict Resolution
- Thinking
- Influencing

The information I share here is not designed to "label" people, but to help you better understand yourself and those with whom you interact.

These styles and leadership are intertwined. Your styles influence how you lead. Believe it or not, style affects how others perceive you and your leadership ability.

Awareness of your styles will help you better understand yourself and those you lead. Acknowledging and appreciating your preferred styles will empower you to become a more effective leader.

Personality Styles

Hands down, the Jung Typology is my favorite when assessing personality style. It's the precursor to the Myers-Briggs Type Indicator (MBTI)® developed by Katherine Coo Briggs and her daughter Isabel Briggs Myers. It's very popular and may be familiar to you. If you have completed the assessment, please get your copy so you can reference your results as you read this section.

If you have not taken the assessment, or if your results are not handy, I have included a link below to a resource where you can complete the assessment and get your results. You can also use it with your direct reports, but for now, we will focus on how this relates to you.

This personality "test" helps us understand who we are at our core, revealing our natural-born tendencies. It measures the degree to which a person is Extroverted (E) or Introverted (I); Sensing (S) or Intuitive (N); Thinking (T) or Feeling (F); and Perceiving (P) or Judging (J). Refer to the chart included below to get a clearer picture of the dimensions and what this means.

Jung Typology Dimensions

100_____0	0_____100
Extrovert (E)	Introvert (I)
Sensing (S)	Intuitive (N)
Feeling (F)	Thinking (T)
Judging (J)	Perceiving (P)

Because it runs along a "continuum," this assessment measures the degree to which we have a tendency to prefer one dimension over the other.

To take the test, scan the QR Code in the front of the book.

After you have done so, please go to Jung Typology to view instructions for completing the test. (Remember to make a note of your results—there should be four letters, and each letter should have a percentage associated with it.)

Your personality style impacts how you lead. I have used a version of this test a number of times with audiences large and small. The discussions about the results are quite insightful.

For instance, time and time again Introverts confirm that it takes a lot of energy to be around large groups of people. Because they replenish their energy by retreating from people and being alone, they may be perceived as quiet or unapproachable. Because you have people reporting to you, retreating to your office and behind closed doors will not bode well for you. To be effective, you will have to learn how to strike a healthy balance.

Remember, this is not about labeling; it's about learning—learning about yourself and how you engage with others.

Regardless of the personality assessment you use, your personality greatly affects how you lead. That's why it's so important to understand your style. Learn as much as you can about yourself. Learn well. Lead well.

For more on leadership and personality styles, please see the Appendix.

Learning Styles

Leaders are lifelong learners.

Your learning style indicates how you take in information and convert it to useable knowledge. The most basic assessment identifies whether you are a *visual, auditory,* or *kinesthetic* learner.

I was at least six years into my career before I knew my preferred learning style. I was participating in a management training course, and the professor led us through an activity to helped us identify our learning style. The exercise revealed that I am a visual learner, with kinesthetic/tactile as a very close second. Auditory lagged way behind in third place.

It was like a light switch had been flipped and suddenly the room had been flooded with light.

As a visual learner, I tend to think in "pictures." No wonder I talk with my hands and like images that convey meaning. My secondary style, kinesthetic (also known as tactile) means I prefer learning some things hands-on by engaging in activity. In essence, I learn by seeing and doing.

Do you think it would have been helpful to know this information earlier, perhaps as far back as elementary school? I would say so. Once I became aware of my learning style(s) and understood that everyone does not learn the same way, it definitely affected how I would train others.

I find it quite fascinating that you can determine a person's preference just by listening to what they say. The next time you're conversing with someone, see if you can pick up on their learning style. (Even that phrase gives you a hint about my primary and secondary method of learning: *see* and *pick up*.)

Do you know what *your* learning style is? Do you know what it is? If not, take a few minutes to complete a Learning Style Assessment. Scan the QR Code in the front of this book to read more about Leadership and Styles.

Communication Styles

When it comes to communication styles, people tend to be *passive, assertive,* or *aggressive.*

- The **passive person** tends to be indirect and may not express clearly what they are thinking or feeling.
- The **assertive person** tends to give others equal "airtime" to voice their opinions and feelings. They state their opinions and allow others to do the same.
- The **aggressive person** tends to bowl people over and is often described as an "in your face" or "difficult" person to deal with. We all know someone with this style. Perhaps you yourself have been a difficult person at one time or another.

At various times and in varying situations, we all have used each of these styles, but we have a tendency to lead with or lean toward one as our predominate, or preferred, style.

Communication styles directly impact both team and interpersonal interactions. Effective communication moves people to act.

The three styles, along with brief descriptions, are shown below.

Communication Styles

Passive	A person with this style tends to be timid, and even referred to as a "pushover", allowing difficult people to walk all over them.
Assertive	A person with this style is professionally assertive when dealing with people, even people who are difficult. They continue to be open, even if someone disagrees with their opinion.
Aggresive	A person with this style can be difficult to deal with in that they tend to be combative. As a result, others might avoid interacting with this individual.

Let's explore the three styles, the behaviors associated with each style, and strategies for interacting with persons exhibiting these styles.

The person with a **passive communication style** tends to avoid conflict and becomes a "pushover" when they encounter a difficult or highly aggressive person. This person may even feel intimated by a person who expresses their ideas and needs.

Being passive doesn't necessarily mean the person does not have strong opinions; often they do. They are reluctant to voice their opinions, however, either due to fear or what they may consider "out of respect" for the other person. (More on conflict management styles in the next section.)

If this is your preferred style, I encourage you to speak up—especially when you feel strongly about a certain subject or topic. You must be careful not to let your passiveness turn into passive-aggressive behavior. According to Daniel K. Hall-Flavin, MD, of the Mayo Clinic, passive-aggressive behavior is defined as a pattern of indirectly expressing negative feelings instead of openly addressing them.[1]

The person with an **assertive communication style** shares their opinions and needs and is usually interested in hearing the opinion and needs of others with whom they are interacting.

Often, they are direct but not "brutally honest." They are interested in dealing with others with respect and integrity. Even when dealing with a person described as "difficult," they continue to be assertive and professional.

If this describes you: Keep up the good work! Your good example, combined with inviting others to express themselves, will result in more honest conversations and better outcomes.

A person with an **aggressive communication style** tends to "walk all over other people" and doesn't seem to care about listening to others. They are concerned about their own interests and will do what it takes to get what they want, often at the expense of another person.

Needless to say, the person with this style can wreak havoc on team dynamics and may be the cause of unhealthy conflict within a group or organization. This person may be seen as a bully and overbearing since they will make sure their viewpoint is expressed.

If this describes you, it will prove problematic in the long run. Learning to listen will help.

Conflict Management Styles

Conflict tends to "exaggerate" our communication style. If one has a passive communication style, under stress, this person may go further into their "cave" and become less expressive. The aggressive person tends to become more and more overbearing and may "take their marbles and go home" because they are not getting their way.

The conflict management styles listed below are based on the Thomas-Kilmann model developed by Kenneth Thomas and Thomas Kilmann. First published in the 1970s, this model consists of the following styles:
- Forcing
- Withdrawing/Avoiding
- Smoothing
- Compromising
- Problem Solving

As a visual learner who thinks in pictures, I created the image below to show how Kilmann's conflict management styles compare to Stephen R. Covey's six paradigms of human interaction.

Conflict Management Styles

	Assertiveness	
Forcing (Win/Lose)	**Compromising** (Win)	**Problem Solving** (Win/Win)
Withdrawing (Lose/Lose)		**Smoothing** (Lose/Win)

Cooperativeness

As you can see from the X and Y axis, this model considers two dimensions: assertiveness and cooperativeness. Both are measured on a scale of low to high. The various combinations result in the five styles listed above and described below. Overlaying these styles with Covey's Paradigms of

Human Interaction gives deeper meaning and helps us better understand the interworking of these styles.

Forcing—The person who uses this style is very high on asserting their needs and taking care of their interests and concerns, with little to no regard for the person or persons sitting across the table. At this extreme, they exhibit aggressiveness, which destroys any hope of a good working relationship. Forcing compares to Covey's paradigm of "win/lose," which says the way for me to win or get my way is for you to lose.

Smoothing—At the other extreme of Forcing is Smoothing. The person with this conflict management style is so cooperative they will give away everything, especially to a person who assertively demands their way. The person with this style usually compromises to the point that they lose their "voice" because they refuse to assert themselves and express their opinion in a given situation. I liken this style to Covey's paradigm of "lose/win": I am willing to lose so you can win.

Withdrawing—This person avoids conflict altogether. They don't assert their desires, and they don't listen to the desires of the other person. They simply refuse to talk; in essence, they take their marbles and go home. They disengage. By withdrawing from the situation, they avoid effectively dealing with the conflict/disagreement. I liken this style to Covey's "lose/lose." Withdrawing means we both lose when cooperating together is required to get the job done.

Compromising—Compromising is a blend of both assertiveness and cooperativeness. The person wants to "win" but is not necessarily interested in the other person losing. They mean no harm to the other person, but they are not interested in helping them make their case. Compromising is a better choice than either of the previous three styles mentioned above. It takes into consideration the interests of both parties, but it produces inferior results when compared to the next style: Problem Solving.

Problem Solving—Problem solving takes time, but "drop the rock" is time well spent. The person with this style takes into account the interests of both parties and seeks what is in the best interest of all concerned. The problem solver is willing to "drop the rock." In my estimation, this style is akin to what Covey describes as "win/win" and "win/win or no deal" paradigms.

This style requires that a person is concerned about their own interests *and* the interests of the other person. As Covey states, "Win/Win is a belief in the Third Alternative. It's not your way or my way, it's a better way, a higher way." Indeed, problem solving is "a better way, a higher way", when approaching conflict between two parties who must work together to achieve maximum success.

> **DROP THE ROCK**
>
> The first step in resolving unhealthy conflict requires someone to "drop the rock."
>
> Dropping the rock means that at least one party in a conflict stops fighting the other person and is willing to press for what Stephen Covey calls a "Win/Win."
>
> Some would call it taking the high road. I call it taking the road that leads out of a messy situation and using precious energy to produce a better outcome. Rather than fighting the other person over who is right or wrong, it's taking steps to do what is right (for yourself and for the parties involved).
>
> Resolving unhealthy conflict requires being assertive and cooperative; it's sharing your thoughts and ideas as well as listening to the other person's thoughts and ideas, even when you disagree. It is possible to disagree without being disagreeable.
>
> It may take two to tango, but it only takes one to "drop the rock."

I discuss this topic in more detail in Step 3 when I describe how conflict impacts team dynamics. Managing conflict effectively is vital to the health of your team.

Thinking Styles

I am no expert on brain dominance, but I have had the pleasure of sitting in the room with someone who is. I have also listened to others who have done extensive research on this topic. According to my research, a person has a natural preference for processing information on either the left side or the right side of the brain. This doesn't mean they only use one side of their brain. They use both, but they have a preference for one or the other. Hence, a person is said to be either left brain or right brain thinkers.

Left brain thinkers are analytical, pay attention to details, and like to make plans. Right brain thinkers, on the other hand, use holistic reasoning, are conceptual, and rely on intuition.

I've learned that left brain thinking dominates in the workplace. That is not hard for me to believe. With almost twenty-five years working in publicly traded companies, in my experience left brain thinkers tended to reap higher rewards than right brain thinkers.

Thinking Styles and Types of Followers

Although I talk more about followers in Step 3, I think it's necessary to mention Dr. Robert E. Kelley's work on the thinking styles of followers. This and his other works are quite fascinating. But for purposes of this discussion, my focus in on what Kelley calls *types of followers*. The five types are:

1. Sheep
2. "Yes" People
3. Alienated
4. Survivor
5. Effective

At first blush, Sheep and "Yes" People are unappealing, but please bear with me. As a leader, I have encountered all five of these types. Quite frankly, over the course of my career, I have *been* all of these types—or at least behaved like all of them.

The types are measured along two dimensions: Active versus Passive and Independent versus Dependent. I've provided a visual representation, along with a description of each.

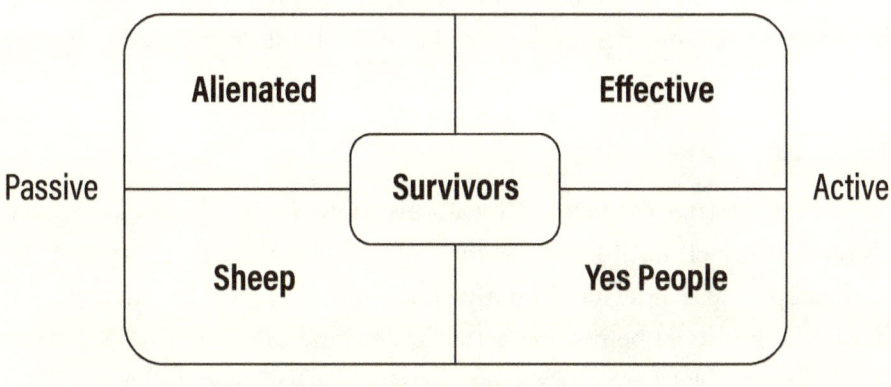

Suffice it to say, we do not all think alike. As a leader, it will serve you well to just admit that other people think differently than you do, including those who report to you. As someone once said to me, "If we both thought the same, one of us would not be needed."

Influencing Styles

Influence is the art of persuasion. It is the "process of affecting the thoughts, behavior, or feelings of another person."[2]

There's a reason I included this last on the list of styles. As a leader, it may be tempting to jump in feetfirst to learn about leadership styles before you're aware of your styles. At least, that was the case for me.

As a new leader, my job was to get work done through others. And since influencing others is how leaders make that happen, my initial focus was on how I could persuade or influence others to do what I needed them to get done.

But in many ways, this was like putting the cart before the horse. My primary focus needed to shift, first learning how I was influenced or persuaded. When I better understood the process of how my thoughts, behavior, or feelings were affected, I was more inclined to seek first to understand others.

Now that you have more information about your styles, I will discuss how they affect your preference for one of the leadership styles identified in Step 3.

Summary

Are you asking yourself, "Why all this about styles?" I used to wonder about that myself until I realized that my individual styles influenced my leadership style. Understanding myself and accepting the fact that people have differing styles helped me better understand others.

Different. Not better or worse. Not good or bad. Just different.

You are in transition, and transitions can be tricky. Transitions can also be stressful. Knowing your styles will help you better navigate tricky and stressful situations, especially one like taking a leap into a leadership position.

Not understanding others, especially those you lead, can stall or stop your career. Understanding yourself and others is one of the keys to your success as a leader.

NEXT STEPS

Now that you know more about styles, see if you can identify your styles.
- Personality
- Learning
- Communication
- Conflict Resolution
- Thinking
- Influencing

Please keep the information you discovered about your styles top of mind as you learn and grow in your new leadership position.

The real voyage of discovery consists not in seeking new landscapes but in having new eyes.
—**Marcel Proust**

CHAPTER 6

KNOW YOUR READINESS FOR YOUR ROLE

No doubt, you are the right person for this position, and it is the right time for you to step up to supervisor. In many ways, this assignment will stretch you.

Did you know that stretching is the only way to grow? Just ask any athlete. Stretching is critically important because it expands their range of motion. Now that you are being stretched, you need to know your readiness for this new range of motion you will be expected to perform.

SWOT Analysis

I have found the SWOT analysis to be an excellent tool. It provides a snapshot of your strengths, weaknesses, opportunities, and threats (which is how the acronym SWOT was derived).

In some ways, it's like a balance sheet that provides a snapshot in time of an entity's assets, liabilities, and equity. The SWOT will help to identity your strengths (assets) and weaknesses (liabilities) to take advantage of opportunities and minimize threats.

Often used in strategic planning, the SWOT can be used in a variety of ways with individuals, teams, and organizations. To better understand it and how it can benefit you in your new role, please take a look at the following explanations.

It's unclear who created this matrix, but it is clear that the letters represent the following:

    S = Strengths
    W = Weaknesses
    O = Opportunities
    T = Threats

This model can guide a leader like you in identifying internal strengths and weaknesses so you can take advantage of external opportunities and diminish potential threats. This process can be used for your team as well, but I encourage you to start with yourself first. I will talk about application to your team in Step 3.

Strengths

Once a goal or objective is identified, it's important to understand the strengths that will assist or aid in achieving that goal. In this case, your mission is to identify how you can be successful in achieving the goals you discussed with your boss in Step One. Take into consideration all the experiences, skills, and knowledge that give you an advantage in being successful in your new position.

Strengths are positives, those skills and abilities that are "good now" and serve to propel you to success. Said another way, strengths represent assets on your personal balance sheet.

Weaknesses

Conversely, weaknesses are those things that are "bad now" and could become liabilities. They work against you and could prevent you from achieving your desired outcome.

You don't want to overemphasize your weaknesses, but you don't want to ignore them either. It's important to assess them accurately because in doing so, you can identify what to do to minimize their impact.

Just so you know, we all have weaknesses. They represent areas for improvement. As a new leader, you are learning to lead. And learning always involve failing. I don't like making mistakes, but there are times when I failed. Never failing is not the goal—that leads to inertia. *Failing up* is the goal. In the words of Dale Carnegie, the goal is to develop success from failure.

Opportunities

Opportunities are those situations that could make for a better future. To take advantage and realize the benefit of these opportunities means that you must seize them in a timely manner. Otherwise that window of opportunity will close.

A TV advertisement for a very famous brand states: "When opportunity knocks and he is not at home, opportunity waits." In reality, opportunity waits for no one.

> *The opportunity of a lifetime must be seized within the lifetime of the opportunity.*
> **—Leonard Ravenhill**

Now is the best time to seize your opportunity of a lifetime. Lay the ground work that increases the chance of success in this particular leadership position.

Threats

Threats, if you are unaware of them and leave them unattended, can severely impact your future success and cause trouble. Plans must be implemented to demolish, or at least diminish, the danger of these threats. Countering threats as they arise, will significantly improve your chances of success.

> *The greatest and most common peril of leadership is that of disqualifying oneself from the position of leadership.*
> **—Dr. Myles Monroe**

Threats are lurking everywhere. Do not let the fact that they are present cause you to disqualify yourself. Let your awareness aid you in putting together a plan to lessen the impact of your threats.

Practical Application

Now that I have covered some details of this model, it's time to talk about its practical application. Take a moment to identify the main takeaways or key points. How could this model be applied in your new job to help you reach your goals?

Could completing a SWOT analysis for your situation possibly improve the likelihood of success? I believe it could.

I often use this model when working with clients to help them assess what they have, what they need, and how they can improve the likelihood of meeting or exceeding a specific goal. I find it most helpful for myself as well, and I think through this process at least on an annual basis. This is never one and done. You will continue learning, growing, and reaping the benefits for your actions.

I really like tools that are simple yet powerful. If you are like me, you will probably want to know more. Scan the QR Code at the front of this book to get information that will be helpful in understanding and applying the model.

Your 90 Day Plan

The guidance included in *Called to Lead* is designed to help you ramp up the learning curve during your first 90 days as a new leader. In some ways it may feel as if you're drinking water through a firehose, but don't panic. You won't drown. As I mentioned in chapter 1, I am a big fan of *The First 90 Days* by Michael D. Watkins. I found it valuable in creating a detailed framework for ramping up the learning curve during the first ninety days in your new position. It contains critical success strategies for new leaders. As you're building your library of resources, this book is one I would highly recommend.

Summary

Remember that you have to pace yourself as you move into your new position of leadership. You will have a long list of to-dos. At the top of the list should be completing a SWOT analysis and laying out the plan for your first ninety days.

Even if you write it on a notepad or the back of an envelope, just writing things down on paper helps to get it out of your head so you can see it more clearly.

The information you put together for your SWOT should be discussed with your boss. Getting input and discussing it with them will be valuable to both of you. It helps your boss become familiar with the way you think and understand how to best help you be successful in your new position.

NEXT STEPS
- Complete a SWOT Analysis
- Lay Out 90 Day Plan

CHAPTER 7

KNOW YOUR RELATIONSHIP WITH YOUR BOSS

I'll let you in on a secret: Cultivating a solid working relationship with your boss is a very good thing. The two of you will be working closely together toward common goals; therefore, building a good relationship is a must.

Your boss is a key link in the chain to your career success. Your performance in this position will set the stage for your next move. (No pressure!)

Cultivating a good rapport with your supervisor sets the stage so you know when things are going right and when they are not.

I read an interesting article entitled "4 Things You Can Say to Make Your Boss Love You"[3] by Dominque Rogers. The four things are:

1. How can I help you achieve your goals?
2. I saw this wasn't done, so I did it.
3. I agree . . .
4. I'd be happy to do that.

Know What Your Boss Expects

What your boss expects may be unclear to you. If this is the case, the burden falls on you to uncover what he or she expects of you. You can bet that your boss expects you to do a great job but sometimes may find it dif-

ficult to express in words what "doing a great job" means. I've discovered that expectations come in several forms:
- Written and unwritten
- Spoken and unspoken
- Known and unknown

Have you ever heard it said that sausage making is not pretty? Well, I've visited a meat processing plant, and I would say that's a major understatement, especially for the one being put to the meat grinder. In some ways, discussions also may be like pulling teeth, difficult to reach, but at the end of the day, the result of the process will be worthwhile.

A leader brings out the best in themselves and others.

Written, Spoken, and Known Expectations

These expectations are the easiest to identify since they are written, spoken, or known. They are included in your job description, company policies, and communicated during meetings with your boss. Because you have tangible evidence of what is expected of you in your new position, they serve as a foundation for two-way communication between you and your boss.

Find out as much information as possible as soon as possible after accepting your leadership position. Knowing what is expected will help you develop your plan for success.

Unwritten, Unspoken, and Unknown Expectations

Expectations that are unwritten *and* unspoken are **unknown** to you. Not meeting **unknown** expectations that are important to your boss can make the difference between survival and success.

The best way to uncover unwritten, unspoken, and unknown expectations is to engage in dialogue with your boss. Schedule a meeting to discuss your position description and the goals you have developed for the next thirty, sixty and ninety days.

When you meet, get agreement from your boss that the two of you are on the same page regarding what is expected. Ask if you are meeting expectations. Follow up by asking what you could do to exceed expectations.

As unwritten, unspoken, and unknown expectations are revealed, make sure to write them down. You can use the Expectations At Work worksheet in the Appendix to record what is expected of you.

Schedule periodic updates to confirm that you know what your boss expects and discuss progress made to date.

Ferreting out what your boss expects will let you know what is most important to him or her, giving you clues on how to prioritize what needs to get done and when. Although it is impossible to write down everything that is expected, it is reasonable to write down and discuss those things that are important.

If you don't know what your boss expects, you stand a fifty-fifty chance of *not* meeting those expectations. My goal is to help you increase your odds of meeting and exceeding expectations by using a proven process of discovery.

TALK TO YOUR BOSS

When my husband was growing up, his Grandmother Tucker owned a salon, Tucker's Beauty Nook. (I like that name.)

This was their tagline: "If your hair is not becoming to you, you should be coming to us."

Now . . . I *really* like that! (Smile!)

You may be asking yourself, "Why is she telling me this?"

I'm glad you asked! This is why: When it comes to knowing what your boss expects, "if your boss has not been talking to you, you should be talking to your boss."

Some folks push back when they hear this. Here's why:

1. Due to their level of experience it's not necessary (they believe they already know).
2. The boss is hard to talk to (not open or doesn't listen).
3. They are not sure what their boss might say.

> Sound familiar? (Some people can relate to more than one.)
>
> Regardless of the reason, it is a fact that review time is coming (sooner or later). You'll have to talk to your boss then. Why not start now?

Know Your Boss's Styles

In Step One you discovered that different people have different styles. That holds true for your boss as well.

Just as your styles affect how you lead your direct reports, this applies to your boss too. Therefore, it will be important to get an idea of your boss's following styles:

- Personality
- Learning
- Communication
- Conflict Resolution
- Thinking
- Influencing

Just observing and listening to your boss will give you some insights.

Because it can be difficult to understand what questions to ask, I have created a Boss Relationship Assessment that you can find by scanning the QR Code at the front of this book.

> ### BE BRIEF. BE BRIGHT. BE GONE.
> *Status is reachable Gwendolyn J. Tucker*
>
> Shortly after I started working for a former boss, I walked into his office, and these are the very words he said: "Be Brief. Be Bright. Be Gone."
>
> Needless to say, I was surprised by his "greeting." And I can honestly say it set me back on my heels. It wasn't that I didn't understand every word he said—I did. I just didn't like the way he said it.
>
> I realized right then and there that this could be a potentially rocky relationship. My personality and his style clashed . . . in a BIG way. So I made it my business to

understand not only what he said, but what he really meant. And this is what I came to believe:

Be Brief: Get your message across as efficiently as possible. Get to the point, tell me what you need, and how I can help.

Be Bright: Give me your best. Show me you've thought through what you're going to say and can get your message across clearly.

Be Gone: Time is a very precious resource. Say what you're going to say and go about taking action on what we discussed.

When I began to look at his comments in this way, it took away some of the "sting," and I stopped taking his words personally. Does that mean I learned to like his direct, brusque style? No, not at all, but I learned to adapt. Finding out what my boss expected was important to me, both in navigating our relationship and for my long-term career.

What your boss expects may be unclear. If this true for you, there are ways to uncover what he or she expects.

Summary

It bears repeating: If you do not know what your boss expects, you stand more than a fifty-fifty chance of *not* meeting expectations. My goal is to help you increase your odds of meeting and/or exceeding expectations by using a proven process of discovery. One of the best things you can do for yourself and your team is to find out what your boss expects. Leaving it to chance only makes things unclear.

NEXT STEPS

It is very possible that your supervisor will take the lead on these discussions. But if not, find a day and time to meet with him or her. Include the purpose of the meeting, which is to discuss and clarify expectations. To prepare for this meeting, complete:
- What Your Boss Expects Worksheet
- Boss Relationship Assessment

STEP 3: PREPARE THE TEAM

Once you have clarity about what is required of you as the new leader, it's time to get your team up to speed. You've talked with your boss about what is expected of you, and you're clear on your goals and objectives. Now it's time to get buy-in from the team.

What I have included in Step Three are the key ingredients for getting your team up to speed so you can achieve what you have been brought together to accomplish.

CHAPTER 8

WORKING WELL TOGETHER (TEAM SWOT)

As you step into the role of leading the team, to achieve any worthwhile goals you must learn to work well together. It's easy to start issuing orders and making assignments, but your first step should be to get to know the people you are leading.

We've covered the importance of knowing the resources you've been given to get your job done. Your human resources—the people who report to you—are your most valuable and appreciable assets.

By now, you have met with your direct reports, started to get to know who they are, what they expect, and what they bring to the table. You have reviewed their résumés or employee records to gain a better understanding of their education, past experiences, what they do well, and what areas need improvement.

With that information in hand, it's time to complete a SWOT analysis for the team. You can complete one on your own, which I recommend. But a powerful team-building exercise is for you and your team members to complete the exercise together. If you are new to the group, your team members have a body of knowledge about the team's capability based on past experience. The SWOT analysis can be completed for each individual team member, and for the team as a whole.

Team SWOT

Some team members may not be familiar with SWOT, and that's okay. This presents an opportunity for the team to learn something new together and develop their critical thinking skills. It also gives you an opportunity to see team dynamics at play and understand the degree to which the team is currently working well together.

Just as a refresher, SWOT gives you the opportunity to identify, discuss, and put in writing the following:

- **S** = Strengths
- **W** = Weaknesses
- **O** = Opportunities
- **T** = Threats

Summary

Identifying strengths and weaknesses for the team gives space for discussing how to best take advantage of opportunities and minimize potential threats. When this process is used with your team, it can be used to foster buy-in and build team collaboration.

Reviewing the outcome of the team SWOT periodically will help ensure the team members are on the same page and working toward mutually beneficial goals.

NEXT STEPS

Using the S.W.O.T. Analysis worksheet in the Appendix:
- Complete S.W.O.T. Analysis for each team member
- Complete Team S.W.O.T. Analysis
- Gain Agreement on Next Steps

CHAPTER 9

BUILDING HIGH-PERFORMING TEAMS

The signature of the best teams is the outcomes they produce.

In your role as leader, getting individuals to work well together is not just a plus, it's a must. It will be in your best interest to develop and execute strategies for building a high-performing work team. Doing so requires you to better understand how teams form and become high-performing teams.

Stages of Team Development

Leadership and team building go hand in hand. This is the way you will get the results you most desire. It is imperative for new leaders to understand the stages of team development *before* the work commences.

As I've mentioned, I'm fascinated by certain models and frameworks. Dr. Bruce W. Tuckman, who conducted research on the Stages of Team Development, does not disappoint. I refer to this information in most, if not all, of the sessions I lead on team building. Dr. Tuckman identified the first four stages (Forming, Storming, Norming, and Performing) in his work published in 1965. Adjourning, the fifth and final stage, was added in 1977.

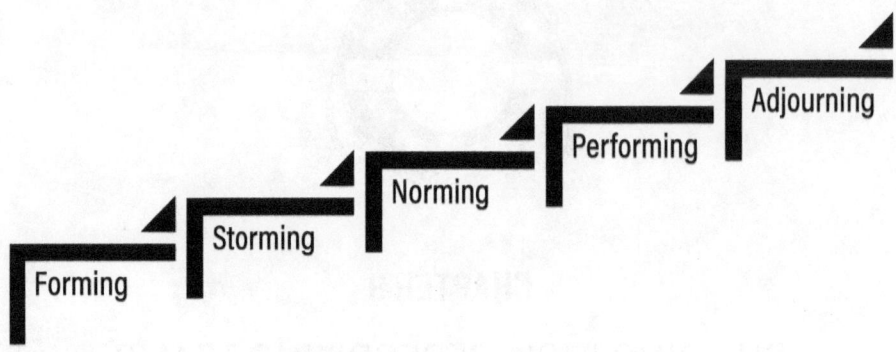

Stages of Team Development

Groups must move through at least the first four stages because all are necessary. As the leader, your role will vary in each stage.

Forming

In its purest state, forming occurs when a group of individuals come together. But in reality, forming (or reforming) occurs whenever a member exits or enters the group.

During this stage, leadership is critical in bringing individuals together to work well as a team. It's in this stage that the purpose of the team, roles, responsibilities, and expectations are discussed. Team members tend to be polite and avoid conflicts during this stage. In this stage, leadership and team building serve as a stabilizing force.

Understanding not only the task before the team but also helping each team member understand the part they play will cultivate an attitude of teamwork and allow them to get to know one another better.

Your responsibility as leader is to clearly communicate goals and objectives; create a positive environment where members accept and commit to accomplishing those objectives; and cultivate trust and foster an environment of cooperation.

Storming

The next stage of team development is *storming*. During this stage, politeness tends to wear off, especially when group members disagree, which means that conflict will arise and be evident.

When two or more people come together, conflicts are inevitable. But unhealthy conflict can derail the team and the task at hand if not addressed. Acknowledging and openly discussing conflict when it arises can help the team immensely. During this stage, the leader must take steps to help the team effectively work through conflict.

This is the most difficult stage of the team building process; it's challenging for both the leader and team members. Unfortunately, some teams get stuck here, and this severely affects their ability to deliver expected results. The actions you take as the leader during this stage can definitely help the team move to the next level.

You do not want to get stuck in storming. Learning how to resolve conflict as it arises is how to have victory over conflict.

Norming

If you are successful at leading your team in navigating stormy waters, you will land on the shores of *norming*. This is when the team starts to "click" and work well together. Signs of progress appear. Dysfunction diminishes. (See the Appendix for more info about the dysfunctions of a team.) Conflicts arise, but they are addressed and actually used to help the team move forward to the next stage of the team's development. Actions taken by the leader during the team-building process begins to pay off and the team becomes more productive.

Performing

Performing! This is the sweet spot—the stage for which you have longed. Your leadership has paid off: Both you and the team are realizing some return on your investment. This is where the team starts working at their optimum, at their best.

Team members proactively solve problems as they arise. There is high respect for one another, and differences are handled appropriately.

Your leadership is critical in getting to and maintaining performance during this stage of team development.

Adjourning

Many teams remain intact, but for cross-functional and ad hoc teams, *adjourning* is a reality. These teams are formed with the intention that they will be dismantled once the task is completed.

Even when teams have a set "end date," the leader's role in building the team is just as (or maybe more so) important. Work must be done in a defined period of time, requiring the group to quickly "gel" together, effectively move through the stages of team development, and work as a high-performing team.

Although most teams don't formally "adjourn," a new team is formed every time a team member exits or enters. In essence, the former team no longer exists, and the new team must progress through the stages of team development.

Adjourning allows you to celebrate accomplishments and formally say your good-byes. It is because of your leadership and ability to build a productive team that you can now celebrate success.

A leader brings out the best in themselves and others.

Summary

As you can see, leadership is critical at each stage of the team's development. Becoming a productive work team requires the group to overcome obstacles, especially when conflict arises.

Unfortunately, most leaders and teams do not devote adequate time and attention to becoming a high-performing work team. But when they do, great success is the reward. They fall prey to the five dysfunctions of a team.

Leadership and team building play a critical role in all stages of group development. To broaden your knowledge, Dr. Tuckman's work on the Stages of Group Development as well as Patrick Lencioni's 5 Dysfunctions of a Team provides helpful insights.

Conflict Management Styles

Conflict tends to "exaggerate" our communication style. If one has a *passive* communication style, under stress this person may go further into their "cave" and become less expressive. The *aggressive* person tends to become more and more overbearing and may "take their marbles and go home" because they are not getting their way.

The conflict management styles listed below are based on the Thomas-Kilmann Conflict Model developed by researchers Kenneth Thomas and Ralph Kilmann. First published in 1974, this model consists of the following styles:
- Forcing
- Withdrawing/Avoiding
- Smoothing
- Compromising
- Problem Solving

Conflict is inevitable when two or more individuals come together. The problem is not that conflict arises. A problem occurs when conflict persists, becomes unhealthy, and is unresolved. For conflict resolution to occur, one party must be willing to "drop the rock."

Definition of Conflict

So, what is conflict? A conflict is a disagreement between two parties. The disagreement can stem from a difference about how certain needs and desires should be met or a difference of opinion. *Merriam-Webster's Dictionary* defines a conflict as "a struggle for power, a difference that prevents agreement; mental struggle arising from incompatible needs, desires, and opinions."

It is very important to note that conflict begins as a mental struggle, which occurs "below the surface." Depending upon the situation and the individuals involved, those involved in a conflict can experience very strong emotions. When handled poorly, conflict becomes very unhealthy and impacts everyone involved—both directly and indirectly.

Conflicts can arise in a variety of situations in the workplace—with the boss, a peer, different departments, etc. Since conflict is inevitable, it is important for leaders and team members to develop skills to "nip" unhealthy conflict "in the bud." This is often difficult; as Lee E. Hood said, "It can be like unscrambling an egg."

Managing Conflict

Wikipedia describes conflict management as "the process of limiting the negative aspects of conflict while increasing the positive aspects of conflict." It is possible to make conflict work for you instead of against you.

As a leader, it is important to become acquainted with the various conflict management styles. First, this will determine your preferred style. Second, it will help you to determine what steps you can take to improve your skills in this area. And third, it will help your team to successfully manage conflict as it arises. Leadership and conflict resolution go hand in hand.

Individuals have varying methods for addressing conflict; these range from avoiding it to effectively resolving conflict. Since conflict is inevitable, developing skills for managing conflict is critical to success: both to you as a leader and for your team. Developing skills to manage and resolve conflict will help you get and stay ahead of the game.

If you haven't done so already, please review the Conflict Management Styles and assess your preferred style. Often, it is easy to judge ourselves based on our intent, while judging others based on their actions or behaviors. Therefore, talking with a trusted colleague about your self-assessment will provide you with a more objective opinion regarding your assessment.

The conflict management style we choose can depend upon the situation and the person(s) involved. For instance, when dealing with a person in authority we may be more cooperative and less assertive.

Steps for Managing Conflict

To better understand your strengths and weaknesses in this area, it is important to understand the process for handling disagreements. My natural personality is toward harmony and peace, which means I have a tendency to avoid conflict. Now, it is good to not intentionally create conflict, but avoiding conflict can be detrimental to healthy working relationships.

> *You need cooperation among people or groups of people to achieve maximum success.*
> —Stephen R. Covey

Michael Maccoby and Tim Studder, authors of the book *Leading in the Heat of Conflict*, have identified the following five steps for managing conflict:

- Anticipate
- Prevent
- Identify
- Manage
- Resolve

Step 1—Anticipate

Since conflict is inevitable when two or more parties come together, anticipate it so you won't be surprised when a difference of opinion occurs. As you are anticipating conflict, prepare yourself with strategies for resolving it. Take into consideration the person with whom you will be dealing and the current state of your working relationship (is it positive or negative).

Fair Fighting Ground Rules may prove helpful in identifying strategies to prevent/minimize unhealthy conflict.[4]

Step 2—Prevent

Prevention is the best cure, but in reality, all disagreements cannot be prevented. However, it is possible to prevent conflict from becoming unhealthy by acknowledging it and seeking to resolve it. The focus should be on preventing conflict from getting out of hand. The best way to do that is to acknowledge and address conflict as it surfaces.

Step 3—Identify

Identify conflict for what it is. Instead of ignoring the "elephant in the room," acknowledge that a disagreement exists. It may feel uncomfortable, but not admitting that the conflict exists provides the fuel for it to grow, not diminish.

Conflict usually arises when the parties have opposing opinions and/or different interests. Getting the parties talking about their concerns and not the conflict can help identify underlying interests.

Step 4—Manage

Managing in the midst of disagreements requires that you acknowledge the underlying interests and emotions of the parties. Maccoby and Studder assert that conflict is emotional. Although the various parties may believe the conflict is based on principle and reason, emotion is involved and should be acknowledged.

Step 5—Resolve

Resolving conflict takes time and skill. It requires that both parties work toward resolution. When conflict is not resolved, count on it surfacing again and again, possibly in a more aggressive or intense manner.

When handled poorly, conflict can impair team dynamics and negatively affect the innerworkings of the team. It will be very important that you as the leader recognize when unhealthy conflict threatens the team and take action to minimize the threat.

Conflict can occur at multiple levels:
- Individual
- Group
- Organization

Learn to recognize the nature of the conflict and develop appropriate strategies for resolving conflict—both within and between the individual, group, or organization.

NEXT STEPS

After observing the team's interaction, you will be able to get an idea of whether the team is working well together. Talk with them about your observations and ask for their feedback. Talk with your team about:
- The Stages of Teams
- Conflict Management Styles
- The Five Dysfunctions of a Team

CHAPTER 10
MOTIVATING YOUR TEAM

To adequately discuss the topic of motivation, I will start with theories of motivation from the perspective of the leader. I would like to highlight what managers believe about employees because what managers believe about their employees (and why they choose to work) directly affects how a supervisor interacts with that employee.

Douglas McGregor was a professor at the MIT Sloan School of Management. He developed the following theories, which were published in his book *The Human Side of Enterprise* in 1960.

Theory X and Theory Y

These theories relate to a manager's belief about what motivates humans and why people work.

Theory X makes negative assumptions about why employees work, whereas Theory Y assumes that employees work for positive reasons, not just selfish reasons.

Each manager makes assumptions about what motivates employees. But their assumptions lead to very different behavior and interaction with employees.

Theory X

The manager who holds the views of Theory X generally believes that employees are lazy and want to avoid work. As such, this manager closely supervises his/her employee's work and often micromanages. This manager believes that employees must be externally motivated to do what needs to be done because the employee has little to no internal motivation to do good work.

Even if an employee is not lazy and does not try to avoid work, the manager who thinks they do will micro-manage the employee.

The manager who subscribes to Theory X believes employees are irresponsible and only work for the money. This manager tends to keep a very tight rein on employees. They believe "the stick" is the best way to keep employees in line. This manager believes that employees will only do a good job if they are externally motivated.

Theory Y

The manager who subscribes to Theory Y believes their employees want to work, are self-motivated, and are responsible. As such, the manager interacts with employees in a different, more positive manner than the Theory X manager.

This manager creates a climate of trust and communicates well with his/her employees, resulting in a more highly engaged workforce.

Summary

The difference between a Theory X and Theory Y manager is what the manager believes about an employee and what motivates them to do what they do.

In essence, the Theory Y manager is often referred to as a leader, not just a manager. This is the type of leader most people want to work for and with.

What motivates you to do what you do? What motivates your direct reports to do what they do? Do you assume they have to be micromanaged in order to get something done? What leadership style would produce the results you most desire?

In a nutshell, Theory X managers believe individuals are motivated by lower order needs. Whereas Theory Y managers believe individuals are motivated by higher order needs. For a more in-depth view on motivation, let's take a look at Maslow's Hierarchy of Needs.

Maslow's Hierarchy of Needs

The Hierarchy of Needs explores Maslow's theory of human motivation and its relevance in the workplace.

I have always been intrigued by human behavior, that of others as well as my own. This theory helps explain, to a certain extent, why people do what they do. It is not designed to be used in a vacuum, but it's a great backdrop by which to better understand others—both at home and in the workplace.

Abraham Maslow was an American psychologist who became famous for creating this theory. He was a professor at several institutions and developed this model back in 1943. The theory asserts that only unmet needs motivate behavior.

Recently I took our vehicle in for maintenance. While there, I had the opportunity to meet the mechanic. I asked her if she enjoyed doing what she does, how she got started, and so on.

She said, "I get to learn about Toyotas, but at the end of the day, cars are like people. They may look different on the outside, but they're the same on the inside."

I thought, *Wow! What an analogy!*

Now, I know that people are different, but I also know that there is something that is the same for everyone: We all have needs. We may meet those needs in different ways, but at the end of the day, we all have needs. That includes you and the people with whom you interact on a daily basis.

Hierarchy of Needs Explained

Initially, Maslow identified five needs in his hierarchy. The sixth, Self-Transcendence, was added later.

These needs are often divided into two categories:
- D-Needs (Deficit)
- B Needs (Being)

The needs are shown below and described in ascending order (from bottom to top).

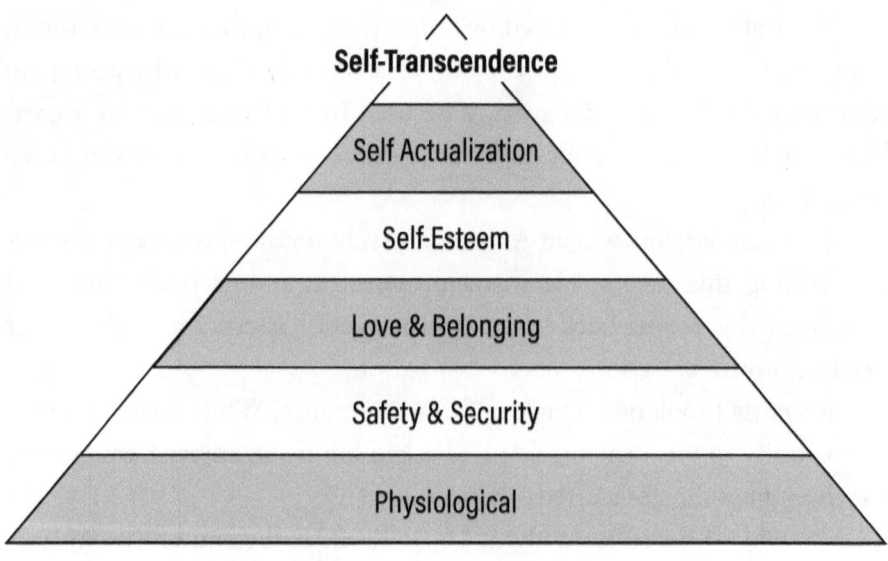

Maslow's Hierarchy of Needs

Physiological

Air, water, and food are needed to survive. I think you would agree. These represent physical needs that *must* be met. Without them, the human body cannot function. In addition, clothing and shelter are necessary to protect humans from the elements such as cold and heat. These needs are the most important and must be met first.

Safety

According to Maslow, when physical needs are satisfied, an individual seeks to address their need for safety. This includes personal and financial security, including health and well-being. This is why people seek job security: it is a way for them to buy the things they need and want. (Many people think that money motivates, but I believe people are motivated by what money can buy.)

Love and Belonging

Love and belonging are social needs. Since "no man is an island," we were not meant to live in isolation. We need other people, and they need us. This is true in the workplace because we must work well together to achieve our goals.

Esteem

This need addresses the desire to feel respected. It includes being respected by others, as well as having a healthy level of self-respect. It revolves around the desire to be accepted and valued by others. In the workplace, being asked to share your idea often results in feeling valued and respected. Seeing your idea put into practice brings a greater degree of satisfaction.

Self-Actualization

Self-actualization refers to being your best possible self in a given situation. It includes being and doing what you believe you were born to be and do. This results in you realizing your full potential.

Transcendence

Most variations of Maslow's Hierarchy of Needs do not list Transcendence separately. According to Maslow's Theory, this need goes beyond the self to satisfy needs greater than oneself. In some circles it is referred to as *generativity*: the concern for others and the desire to contribute to future generations.

Summary

Unmet needs can lead to conflict in relationships, both inside and outside of the workplace.

You may be asking yourself what does this have to do with leadership? My reply: A lot! Understanding what motivates your direct reports and helping them find the WIIFM (What's in it for me?) is a key to gaining buy-in and keeping your team engaged.

Employee Engagement

There is much talk these days about employee engagement or the lack thereof. Much research has been done and reports of studies have been, and continue to be, compiled and communicated. Yet, increasingly, more and more workers report that they are not engaged at work—at least not to the degree that they plan to remain with their current employer.

An engaged workforce is vital to success—yours, your organization, and each member of your team. The leader who leads understands the importance of and develops the skills to engage his/her employees.

The "X" Model of Employee Engagement

Buck Blessing and Tod White, pioneers in the field of employee engagement, developed the "X" Model of Employee Engagement Equation:

$$E = C + S$$
(Engagement = Contribution + Satisfaction)

Contribution represents what an employee **gives** and Satisfaction represents what an employee **gets**.

As a leader, you and your organization are highly concerned about contribution (also known as performance or productivity), because you want to get the most "bang for your buck." And it may seem that some workers are more concerned about satisfaction (which you may interpret as doing less). But in reality, you must be concerned about both contribution and satisfaction. These two components must be balanced. If they are too far out of alignment, employee engagement will be negatively impacted.

Everyone plays an important role in achieving an engaged workforce. It is not just the leader's responsibility, nor just the individual employee's responsibility, nor even just the executives' responsibility. No, this is a team effort. Everyone must play their part and play it well.

Here is a suggestion on how to use this information. Start by rating your level of engagement. Would you say you are giving your maximum contribution and getting maximum satisfaction? If not, what can you do to change that?

Next, assess the degree to which the members of your team are giving maximum contribution and receiving maximum satisfaction. Share your assessment with them and determine what actions you will take. Different people are motivated by different things. There is no "one size fits all" when it comes to motivation.

Summary

An engaged workforce is critical to success—yours, your employee's and the organization's. Now is a good time to develop your strategy for building a more engaged and high-performing team. It is the only way to realize the level of success you and your team are capable of achieving.

NEXT STEPS

1. Review Theory X and Theory Y to determine which style you can most relate to.
2. Determine ways to best motivate your direct reports.
3. Identify behaviors which indicate that your team members are engaged.

THE EMPLOYEE GOLDEN RULE

*The secret to a great customer experience is
a great employee experience.*
—Shep Hyken

A lot of focus is placed on customer experience or CX, but not as much on employee experience. That is probably because the customer is seen as a company's bread and butter. And they are.

Well, I stumbled upon a great article in *Forbes* where Shep Hyken discloses the secret to a great customer experience. He starts out by saying, "What happens on the inside of the organization is felt on the outside by the customer." So true.

I really like what he refers to as The Golden Rule for Employees: **"Do unto employees as you want done unto customers."**

I firmly believe that how we treat our employees is reflected in how our employees treat our customers. What would happen in your company if you started treating your employees as internal customers?

What would be the WIIFM (what's in it for me)? According to Shep, the following:

1. Lower employee churn (Who doesn't want to keep good performers?)
2. Built-in brand ambassadors (Happy employees gladly tell others.)

Here's one more: a highly engaged workforce.

My question to you is this: If you conducted a survey today, how would your employees rate their internal customer experience? Would the results show there's room for improvement?

CHAPTER 11

LEADING IN STYLE

Much research has been completed related to leadership theories and models. I tend to be fascinated by theories because they represent a system of principles upon which something is based. Let's look at the theories that have impacted our belief about leadership today. The research continues to evolve and affects our thinking about leadership.

Leadership Theories/Styles

Trait Theory

Leadership Trait Theory dates back to Thomas Carlyle's "Great Man" theory and later research by Galton, which sought to identify leaders based on physical attributes, personality type and abilities. *Natural selection* is the term most commonly used for this theory.

At the heart of this early research is the belief that leaders are born not made—that leaders inherited personal characteristics or traits. If this theory had been proven to be true, leadership would be innate, and leadership could not be developed. Leaders had to be born that way.

Although many things were learned from this research, there are no strong correlations that proved leaders are indeed born that way.

Trait Theory of leadership was widely accepted for more than one hundred years, until it was criticized in the 1950s and strongly challenged in the 1980s.

Behavioral Theories

Out of the weaknesses found in Trait Theory evolved three theories upon which modern leadership theories are founded: Lewin, Ohio State, and the Michigan studies. These theories are commonly referred to as *behavioral theories*.

Lewin Studies

Probably the most popular research on leadership styles was conducted by Kurt Lewin and a team of students. This research has come to be known as the Lewin Studies. Lewin, along with Lippett and White, identified three basic leadership styles: autocratic, democratic, and laissez-faire.

The premise is that a leader uses one of three styles when approaching their direct reports. It further proposes that the style does not change based on the situation but is fixed. The studies concluded that one of these is used when relating to or interacting with their followers.

An autocracy is a system of government in which the decision making is concentrated in the hands of one person—in this case, the person in charge.

The **autocratic leader** tends to be dictatorial; their actions tend to be directive and controlling. Their goal is to enforce the rules and keep a tight rein on workplace activities and relationships. This manager gives the impression that things must be done their way.

Democratic leadership is also referred to as participative leadership_or participative management. This type of leader generally inspires team members, is inclusive, and values the opinions of those he or she is leading. This type of leadership is transformational.

The democratic leader is collaborative, interacts with followers and seeks buy-in concerning decisions about the work and work environment that directly affects the team.

Thankfully, I have worked for this type of leader. They realized that I (and my fellow team members) had talents and used our input to accomplish mutually beneficial goals. They create a "culture of we" not a "culture of me" where the boss is believed to be the only smart person in the room.

Having positive role models helped me develop and become not only a better leader, but a better person. This type of leader brings out the best in their followers.

The **laissez-faire style** is often referred to as "non-leadership." These leaders fail to accept the responsibilities of the position and do not use their influence to create win-win situations. This often results in chaos and loss of respect for the manager. Unfortunately, this behavior negatively impacts everyone connected to the manager with this style.

In addition to your preferred style identified from the Lewin Studies, other "styles" come into play and impacts a leader's ability to get work done through others. These include Personality, Communication, Learning, Conflict Resolution and Influencing.

Contingency Theory

Contingency Theory, also known as Situational Leadership Theory, addresses two factors:
- Leader Style/Behavior
- Follower Maturity or Readiness

Developed by Paul Hersey and Kenneth Blanchard, Contingency Theory is a practical leadership model that, when practiced and perfected, can lead to very positive outcomes for the leader and follower. It is designed to help leaders match their leadership style to the readiness level of the follower in a specific situation. Therefore, the leader learns to adjust their leadership style based on the follower's readiness to complete a task or project. Let me say that again, the leader adjusts his/her style based on the follower's readiness and not vice versa.

I was introduced to this model more than twenty years ago. Of all the leadership theories, it is my favorite. Let me tell you why.

Leader Behavior

According to Hersey and Blanchard, leaders engage in four primary behaviors with their followers:

S1 – Telling/Directing
S2 – Selling/Coaching
S3 – Participating/Supporting
S4 – Delegating

Styles S2 and S3 are high relationship, since the leader focuses on explaining decisions and invites the follower to share ideas.

Styles S1 and S4 tend to be low relationship, but for different reasons. S1 is a hands-on approach where the follower is closely supervised, whereas S4 is "hands off," resulting in the follower having full responsibility for completing the task at hand.

Usually, leaders favor one of these styles more than others. But that practice can cause problems, since the leader's behavior should be adjusted based on the readiness of the follower. This is the **core premise** of this model. Let's look at each style in more detail.

S1 - Telling/Directing

Telling/directing is described as "high task and low relationship." It is prescriptive in nature; the leader gives specific directions/instructions to the follower. This style is used when the follower is inexperienced or low in ability, as it relates to what is required in the situation. For instance, if a follower is responsible for completing a project or task that is relatively new and/or complex in nature, the leader should use this style. In this style, the leader provides close supervision.

S2 - Selling/Coaching

Selling helps the follower "buy in to the process." It involves coaching or guiding and is "high task and high relationship." The leader provides direction and supervision, but also a healthy dose of encouragement. The leader encourages the follower to be involved, serves in the role of coach, and takes time to answer questions and explain decisions.

S3 -Participating/Supporting

This style is "low task and high relationship." The leader enters into a more collaborative role with the follower. Both parties take part in setting objectives. There is "shared decision making," which means the leader involves the follower in decision-making.

S4 - Delegating

Delegating is giving the follower the freedom to determine how the task or project is going to get done. The leader uses this style is used when the follower is capable of delivering and confident they can do so. The leader encourages the follower to take as much responsibility as they can handle. Please note: Delegating does not mean "dumping" tasks you do not like or want to do.

In order for someone to learn, they must step out of their comfort zone.
—Shannon Brown

Summary

Because it focuses on determining the best leadership style for the situation and person(s) involved, the leader is encouraged to develop their ability to use a variety of styles, thus avoiding the pitfalls of a one-style-fits-all approach. Those who harness the power of the Situational Leadership Model will experience positive outcomes for themselves and those they lead.

> **NEXT STEPS**
> Using the Situational Leadership Model, identify your preferred leadership style:
> - Telling/Directing
> - Selling/Coaching
> - Participating/Supporting
> - Delegating

The person who is good with a hammer thinks everything is a nail.

The premise is that effective leaders know how to adapt the appropriate style to the maturity or readiness of a person or group being led. Those who master these concepts realize a high degree of success. Now let's delve a little deeper into understanding Follower Maturity or Readiness levels.

Follower Readiness Levels

According to Hersey and Blanchard, there are four maturity levels:

M1 – Low
M2 – Moderate-Low
M3 – Moderate-High
M4 – High

Maturity, or readiness, has two parts: ability and motivation. Ability includes the skills and understanding to complete the task at hand. Motivation relates to the incentive to accomplish the task and the willingness to assume responsibility.

M1 – Low Maturity Level

The follower with a Maturing Level 1 is described as unable and insecure. This person is low in skill and will. They do not understand the task to be completed, nor are they confident they can complete the task.

If we think hard enough, we can remember a time when we were at this level of maturity in a specific situation. The person rated as M1 has low ability and low motivation. The appropriate leader style is S1 – Telling.

M2 – Moderate-Low Maturity Level

The follower with this level of maturing is willing but unable to take full responsibility without help from the leader. The person with these attributes reminds me of the story of *The Little Engine That Thought It Could*. This person repeats to himself: "I think I can, I think I can!"

M3 – Moderate-High Maturity Level

A follower with readiness level 3 is very capable but low in confidence. You may have worked with someone like this. They are talented, but they don't realize it. They sell themselves short, thinking they can't when in reality they have the skills to do the job and do it well.

The leader should use a supporting style with this follower, one that is low-task but high-relationship.

M4 – High Maturity Level

The person with this maturity level is high in ability and high in motivation. They are up for the challenge and ready to accept full responsibility for success. When this is the case, the leader delegates the task and stays engaged to monitor progress.

Summary

It is very important for you as the leader to determine task-specific readiness. Becoming too dependent on a preferred style will prove detrimental for you and the follower. So remember, leader style must align with follower readiness.

There are four leadership styles that correspond with a follower's maturity or readiness level, which relates to their ability to complete an assigned task. The success of the model rests on matching the appropriate leader style with follower readiness.

CHAPTER 12

COACHING YOUR TEAM MEMBERS

Have you ever heard it said that a leader should be like a coach? If you played organized sports, you know that the coach serves a very important role for the team. Without the coach, the team would surely fail.

As you read this Chapter, seeing your role from the perspective of a coach might change how you approach your direct reports as well as the task at hand.

Unfortunately, too many leaders are thrust into their roles with little or no support for learning how to lead. They tend to be good performers from a technical or functional point of view—they're good at doing the work. But they struggle at getting work done through others.

Leaders must master the basics of managing and measuring work. But before they can do that, the infrastructure of a robust performance management program must be in place. Building a culture of accountability requires that you master the basics.

Managing and Measuring

Managing and measuring work explores the critical components all leaders must master. They are critical to the performance management process and include the following:
- Set Clear Goals and Objectives

- Monitor Progress
- Provide Timely Feedback

Neglecting any of these components will prove problematic at annual review time.

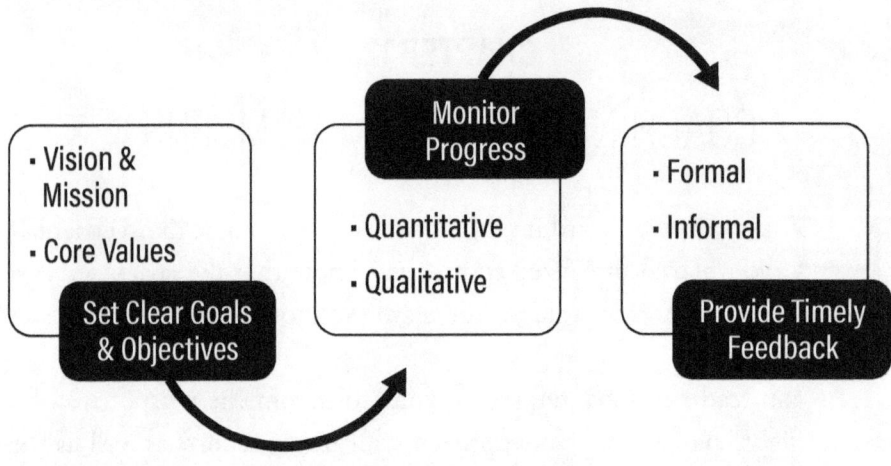

Managing & Measuring Work

As a leader, a major responsibility of your role is to manage and measure work, both yours and those of your direct reports. Therefore, it is incumbent on you to get well acquainted with your company's performance management processes and procedures. Once you are familiar with what is required, it is time to execute what is outlined.

Unfortunately, too many leaders fail to master the skills associated with managing and measuring the work of others. Successful leaders—leaders who lead—understand how important it is to a team's overall performance.

A robust performance management program is foundational to building a culture of accountability and consists of five elements:

1. Purpose
2. Process
3. People
4. Plan
5. Practice

Purpose

Purpose represents the driving force behind why we do what we do. It is our reason for being. Holding yourself (and one another) accountable is easy when we have bought into the Vision, Mission, and Core Values of the organization. Purpose is the big WHY that fuels us and anchors us.

Process

The process outlines "how" work will be managed and measured. And should be contained in your company's policies and procedures manual.

Since it governs how performance will be reviewed, rated and rewarded, you must become well acquainted with the intricacies of this policy.

If you have not read it lately, now is a good time to review it in detail, discuss with your boss and share it with your direct reports.

People

The people are the lifeblood of the organization; without them you have no organization or company or team.

Therefore, your direct reports must be very clear on what is expected and how their performance will be reviewed, rated and rewarded.

Communicating and getting agreement up front will help minimize confusion and conflict later on.

Plan

The plan represents the WHAT—the specific steps you can apply to each person and the timing of when those steps or actions will be taken. For example, as Customer Relationship Manager for the Foodservice Business, I had monthly performance discussions with my boss. But I had quarterly discussions with some of my direct reports. So, the timing and frequency of feedback discussions will vary.

Practice

We've all heard that "practice makes perfect." Well, in reality, *perfect* practice makes perfect. Practice "bakes in" all the elements to create a culture of accountability. This is when you get to practice setting clear goals and objectives, monitor progress, and provide timely feedback, which we'll look at next. It's the "stuff" performance management is made of!

Set Clear Goals

Ideally, goals should be set by the first day of the fiscal year. (For most organizations, the fiscal year coincides with the calendar year that begins January 1.) Doing so gives the individual the full year to accomplish their goals and objectives.

Monitor and Track Progress

Once goals and objectives have been established, you must identify how you will measure what is achieved. They should include both quantitative and qualitative data that will be used to determine what progress has been made toward reaching the goal. This allows you and your direct report to discuss progress against preset goals aligned with the organization's strategic goals and objectives.

Provide Timely Feedback

Providing feedback is very important and should be given in both formal and informal settings. For example, I recommend giving impromptu feedback close to the time the person's performance is observed. If it is positive feedback, I will not hesitate to make my comments in the presence of others. If it is constructive feedback, I recommend sharing that one on one. This is in line with one of Dale Carnegie's principles: "Praise in public. Reprimand in private."

Formally, leaders should meet one on one with each direct report at least quarterly. The purpose of this meeting is to discuss performance: what is going well and what needs to be corrected.

This meeting is also a good time for you, the leader, to ask for feedback on how you can best help and support your direct report in reaching his or her goals. Providing timely feedback allows you to discuss progress at intervals, instead of waiting until it's too late for corrective actions to be taken.

Set Clear Goals and Objectives

> *Leaders know the way, go the way, show the way.*
> —John C. Maxwell

Clear goals and objectives identify what is expected and must include metrics or key performance indicators (KPIs) that tell if or when the goal is reached. You need metrics in order to manage and measure work. Individual (and team) goals and objectives must be aligned with the organization's strategic goals and objectives.

To do this, the organization must identify its goals and communicate them in such a fashion that they are understood to everyone within the organization. If this is not common practice within your organization, there may be a lot of **activity**, but it will not be **productivity**. There is a BIG difference.

Productivity is productive activity; it contributes to the mission and helps to move an organization closer to achieving its mission. Being clear on what is expected *BEFORE* the performance period begins helps set the foundation upon which solid performance can be built. This includes knowing what your boss expects of you.

> *All actions have consequences.*
> —Stephen R. Covey

SMART Goals

Setting SMART Goals is a key step in achieving your dreams. Without them, you are sure to lose focus and get distracted. Adhering to these criteria will help you keep your eye on the prize. SMART goals is an acronym—initially discussed in an article published by George T. Doran and later attributed to Peter Drucker—that identifies criteria for setting objectives:

S = Specific
M = Measurable
A = Achievable
R = Relevant
T = Time-Bound

> *Goals are dreams with deadlines.*
> —Diana Scharf Hunt

S = Specific

Being specific helps to clarify the "what." It helps you begin with the end in mind by clearly defining your purpose or desired outcome. Doing so increases the likelihood that you will hit the target. Why? Because once you know your bullseye, you know where to aim and direct your precious resources.

M = Measurable

This criterion will help you know when the goal is reached. It represents your finish line. Knowing what the end looks like (in measurable terms) also allows you to break it down into smaller pieces or milestones.

A = Achievable

It is one thing to set a stretch goal. But it is demotivating to aim for something you know you cannot possibly reach. If you believe something is impossible, you will not exert the effort to even try. In your mind, it is futile. Failure is not only an option; it is inevitable.

> *Make no little plans. They have no magic to stir men's blood*
> *and probably will not themselves be realized.*
> —Daniel Burnham

R = Relevant

Goals that are irrelevant are unimportant. Because they are not important, there is little or no incentive to achieve them. Precious resources, such as your time, energy, etc., will be devoted to those areas that are of the utmost importance to you. Therefore, they must be closely connected to something that will have a profound effect on your success.

T = Time Bound

Time-bound simply refers to the fact that there must be an "end date." You must establish the date when your goal is "due" to be completed. It answers the question, "By when?" Unless you set a deadline, there is a high likelihood the goal will not be accomplished. So convert your dreams into reality. Write them down, take action on them, and review them often.

Performance Feedback

Feedback is a gift. Performance feedback, both giving *and* receiving it, is critical to growth and development. With it, individuals can succeed. Without it, individuals will surely fail. Since feedback is so critical to success, read on for advice on how to do it well.

Unfortunately, some leaders are unskilled at giving and receiving feedback. This is due, in part, to poor role models and/or lack of coaching on how to give constructive feedback.

It is expected that a leader should give performance feedback to their direct reports, but "best in class" organizations ensure that feedback occurs:
- Peer to Peer
- Leader to Direct Report
- Direct Report to Leader

In essence, feedback is a response to a person's performance of a given task. It should be **constructive, specific, timely, consistent,** and **objective**.

Constructive

Giving positive feedback tends to be pretty easy, but giving constructive feedback can be difficult. Constructive feedback is designed to correct future behavior, not punish the person for past performance. Some managers will readily tell employees what they did wrong or could improve upon. But they neglect to tell their direct report what they did well. They are critical, and their comments are too. Feedback is constructive when it is used as a basis to improve the person's future performance.

> *We're not here to beat you up. We're here to make you better.*
> —**Lee E. Hood**

Specific

When giving feedback, it's important to talk about the issue/situation. Be specific. Do not speak in general terms or make it personal by attacking the other person's character.

I recall a recent situation when a peer did not follow up with me. Their lack of follow-up negatively affected my ability to meet a preset deadline. It was tempting to just "let it go" and not address the situation. But there was unresolved conflict that could potentially impact future interactions.

Although I felt nervous about confronting the person, I was able to do so without being confrontational. I focused on their lack of follow-through and its impact on me and my work.

I felt positive about the outcome, and I think they did too.

Timely

In addition to being constructive and specific, feedback should be given in a timely manner. Although formal performance discussions should occur at least quarterly, feedback should be given close to the time the performance is observed. If the performance feedback is positive, I usually give it at the time I observe it. If it is constructive, I will select a time that works for both parties.

My husband was a Dale Carnegie instructor for several years. According to him, this rule of management is the one to live by: "Praise in public and reprimand in private."

Consistent

Some managers are consistently inconsistent. This behavior negatively affects their credibility. It is very important to be consistent in offering and asking for feedback. Consistency instills confidence in the recipient that whether good or bad, you can be counted on to give your feedback on their performance.

It's also important that you ask for feedback from your direct reports. If you do not get their feedback, how can you determine if you are an effective leader? In my estimation, this is the best way to identify steps you can take to become a leader who leads.

Objective

When giving feedback on someone's performance, it is important to be objective and keep your comments in perspective, especially if the person's performance did not meet expectations. To keep it objective, use the person's job description as your basis for judging/evaluating their performance. Keep your feedback in the context of their job description, what is expected of the person occupying the position, and how well they performed what was expected.

Coaching Conversations

Coaching conversations can be quite powerful, especially for millennials in the workplace. They like to know what is expected and get feedback on their performance in a timely manner to allow them to make adjustments as needed. This applies to all of your direct reports. From day one of your new leadership position, be thinking about how you will communicate with your team members.

Coaching conversations should be conducted at least once per month, maybe more, depending on the role and the tasks at hand. The purpose of the conversation will be to review progress against goals (what's expected) for the month. Together, you and your employee should come up with a plan of action to meet or beat the goals established for the month.

This is an opportunity to ensure expectations are clear. Your people will know where they stand regarding their performance. This minimizes gray areas.

In so many companies, employees do not know what is expected or how they will be evaluated. But coaching conversations ensure that expectations will be set at the beginning of the performance period.

Summary

> *A title and position do not guarantee performance and productivity.*
> —Dr. Myles Monroe

Most leaders love their "star players"—those who take initiative and do what needs to be done without having to be told or minimal prodding. But a true test of leadership requires the willingness and capacity to develop direct reports who need more guidance and hands-on supervision. Note: Hands-on supervision does not mean micromanaging. It means giving your people the support *they* need in a given situation.

Remember, everyone is not the same.

STARR Performance Framework

I developed a process that you as the leader can use to get better outcomes and help you motivate your team to play like all-stars. The STARR Performer Framework identifies five steps required to help your direct reports meet expectations

- **Set Goals** – clarify what is expected at the beginning of the performance period
- **Track/Trend Progress** – monitor progress made along the way at frequent intervals

- **Adjust Accordingly** – make self-corrections in a timely manner to avoid going too far off course
- **Recognize Efforts** – take notice of effort put forth by your people to achieve their goals
- **Reward Results** – at the end of the performance period (usually annually) with monetary awards

For more information and guidance on how to implement the STARR Framework, please see the Appendix.

NEXT STEPS

Identify specific goals and objectives for each of your direct reports.

Schedule a meeting with each of your direct reports to communicate and discuss what is expected. Get their agreement and buy-in.

Lay out a plan for future discussions to give timely feedback on their performance and identify how you can support them in their efforts.

STEP FOUR: PREPARE TO ACHIEVE

In the introduction of this book, I wrote that I consider it an honor that you would not only buy *Called to Lead* but that you would take the time to invest in yourself by reading it. The fact that you have gotten to this point means you took me up on my offer to invest in yourself. You have read about some valuable life lessons that I was taught—and some I caught—along the pathway to becoming the leader I am today. It's now time to put together, in an orderly fashion, all you have gleaned from this text.

CHAPTER 13

PUTTING IT ALL TOGETHER

You've charted the course—now it's time to set sail.

I have outlined these lessons in a way that makes sense to me. Although leadership is both art and science, you are now familiar with the methodology and framework I used to develop my leadership skills and that I encourage my clients to use as well. The steps are interdependent and are intended to be followed in this sequence:

    Step One: Prepare to Succeed
    Step Two: Prepare to Lead
    Step Three: Prepare the Team
    Step Four: Prepare to Achieve

Following these steps will assist you in ramping up the learning curve regardless of the leadership position you are called to take on. I fully believe that relevant information plus rigorous application results in realized transformation. As you take and apply what is contained herein, you will see the fruit of your labor as you become a leader who leads. Know this: I am cheering you on every step of the way.

Conclusion

One of the most exhilarating times of my career was being promoted into a leadership position. It also proved to be very challenging. As you get your arms around what you signed up for, you may be rethinking your decision. That is natural. Pace yourself. Rome was not built in a day.

Instead of looking around in despair, put pen to paper and start writing out your plan on how you will ramp up the learning curve in your new position.

You are not doing this alone. Make sure you write down on your list all the people and other resources you have to get the job done. Your boss should be a helpful resource. Your boss is the one who selected you for your new leadership position and has a vested interest in your success, because it directly impacts his or her success.

Yes, you are the right person. You are in the right place. You are called to lead.

Part II:
LEADERSHIP VAULT

In this part, you'll find a collection of articles I've written that reveal some of my lessons learned on the journey to becoming the leader I am today. There's a famous saying that some lessons are taught, and others are caught. This section contains both.

At times, leading can feel precarious. It seems as if you're looking through a fog, not quite sure how to make out what's right in front of you. The following vignettes will serve as companions to the Steps contained in Part I. My hope is that they will bring the information into focus so that you will see how to apply them in practical ways that are as clear as day.

You will not be surprised that I start off with "Begin with the End in Mind," since I am a *huge* Stephen Covey fan. His book *The 7 Steps of Highly Effective People* is a must-have for every professional, especially those in leadership positions.

Or you might get a chuckle out of reading "Be Brief, Be Bright, Be Gone." I can laugh about it now, but it definitely did not feel good then.

Wherever you start on this list, my hope is that you will find some nuggets of insight and practical tips to add to your tool kit to help you ramp up the leading curve. It would be my pleasure to assist you in becoming the leader you were destined to become.

BEGIN WITH THE END IN MIND

A very good friend of mine reported some great news. She made the highest possible rating on her annual performance review! Needless to say, she was so delighted . . . and so was I! Lots of smiles! High fives! Job "whale" done!

Boy, did we celebrate!

Want to know how she did it? She did what Stephen Covey advised in his book *The 7 Habits of Highly Effective People*. She began with the end in mind.

While discussing her prior year's performance, she asked her boss this question, "What can I do next year to achieve the highest possible rating?"

Based on what she gleaned from that discussion, she set her goals, developed her plan of action, and delivered results—day in and day out.

And you can too. Here's how:

Take a look at your current job description. It should reflect what is expected of you in your role. If it doesn't, get help to update it. Talk with your boss. Find out his/her goals and priorities for the year. Ask how you can contribute. Tell your boss you are serious about exceeding expectations. Then take consistent, deliberate action.

These are the habits of highly effective people. It's very possible that this time next year you could be hearing your boss say, "Congratulations! Your performance consistently exceeds expectations. . . and to go with that, here's your raise!"

Big smile!

BE BRIEF. BE BRIGHT. BE GONE.

Shortly after I started working for a former boss, I walked into his office and heard him say these very words: "Be brief. Be bright. Be gone."

Needless to say, I was surprised by his "greeting." And I can honestly say it set me back on my heels.

It wasn't that I didn't understand every word he said. I did. I just didn't like the way he said it. I realized then and there that this could be a potentially rocky relationship. My personality and his style clashed—in a BIG way. So, I made a decision. I made it my business to understand not only what he said but what he really meant. And this is what I came to believe:

- **Be Brief**—Get your message across as efficiently as possible. Get to the point. Tell me what you need and how I can help.
- **Be Bright**—Give me your best. Show me you've thought through what you're going to say and can get your message across clearly.
- **Be Gone**—Time is a very precious resource. Say what you're going to say and go about taking action on what we discussed.

When I began to look at his comments in this way, it took away some of the "sting," and I stopped taking his words personally. Does that mean I learned to like his direct, brusque style? No, not at all. But I learned to adapt. Finding out what my boss expected was important to me, both in navigating our relationship and for my long-term career.

What your boss expects may be unclear. If this true for you, make a decision to uncover what he or she expects.

MANAGING AND MEASURING WORK

Managing and measuring work is an important part of a leader's role. It requires the following:
- Setting clear goals and objectives
- Monitoring progress along the way
- Giving timely feedback

Unfortunately, too many managers are unskilled at doing these things. On average, six out of ten employees report not having clear goals/objectives or receiving meaningful feedback from their manager in the last six months.

If this describes you, now is the time to talk with your direct reports about how their performance compares with what you expect.

Or if you have not received feedback on your performance within the past three months, there *is* something you can do: Ask for it. Find out now what your boss expects, early and often. Doing so now, rather than waiting until later, will help you understand what you are doing well and what must be improved in order to meet (or exceed) expectations.

ALL ABOARD!

Before the fiscal year begins, you should outline your goals for the year, shared them with your team, and made sure each of your direct reports are onboard. You have outlined your plan and have the meeting confirmed on everyone's calendar. Taking this action now, at the beginning of the year, will help you make sure your team members know:
- What must be achieved
- The part they are expected to play
- How their contribution will be measured

If you haven't done so yet, it's not too late! But don't wait too much longer. "Don't leave your shipmates behind. Make sure they're all aboard!" Neither you nor your team should be left behind. Make sure everyone can say in the affirmative, "All aboard!"

TALK TO YOUR BOSS

When my husband was growing up, his Grandmother Tucker owned a salon: Tucker's Beauty Nook. (I like that name.) This was their tagline: "If your hair is not becoming to you, you should be coming to us." Now . . . I REALLY like that! (Smile!)

You may be asking yourself, "Why is she telling me this?" I'm glad you asked! When it comes to knowing what your boss expects: "If your boss has not been talking to you, you should be talking to your boss."

Some folks push back when they hear this, for a number of reasons. Here's why:
- Due to their level of experience, they feel it's not necessary; they believe they already know.
- The boss is hard to talk to (or not open or doesn't listen).
- They are not sure what their boss might say.

Does this sound familiar? (You might be able to relate to more than one.) Regardless of the reason, it is a fact that review time is coming (sooner or later). You'll have to talk then. Why not start now? Find out what your boss expects!

PASSING MUSTER

It's that time of year! The prior year's performance is evaluated, documented, and communicated.

You are finding out if you pass muster—i.e., whether your performance meets with your boss's approval. If expectations were clearly communicated and ongoing feedback was received during the year, there should be very few surprises. But if that is not the case, there's a high likelihood you will be unpleasantly surprised at performance review time, due to one of two reasons:

- You did not know or you were not crystal clear on what was expected.
- You were not aware that your performance does not meet with your boss's expectations.

So, what should you do? Well, you can't go back and make a new beginning, but you can make a new ending. Here's how: Be open to feedback. But more than that—determine to do something about the things you can control.

Although you may only want to hear the positives, be open to constructive feedback. It is the only way to improve your performance. Do not allow yourself to be caught in this situation again. Begin now to find out what your boss expects. Then ask for feedback along the way.

ILL-EQUIPPED LEADERS

All too often, individual contributors are promoted to leadership positions with little or no guidance on how to be an effective leader.

The one who promoted them may believe this: "If they are outstanding as an individual contributor, they will automatically excel in a leadership position."

So, the individual contributor is promoted. And everyone suffers:
- **The New Leader** no longer realizes the stellar results they are accustomed to achieving.
- **The People They Lead** flounder due to lack of effective leadership.
- **The Person Who Promoted Them** may have second thoughts about their first choice.

But the problem may not be that the individual contributor was the wrong choice. The problem may be that the new leader needs support to develop their ability to get work done through others. The question, though, is how.

Ideally, a senior leader can provide opportunities to develop leadership skills before promoting someone to a leadership position. Realistically, the plan after promotion must include education and training to grow and develop the skills necessary for success in the new role.

Now, some believe that "leaders are born, not made." But the truth is that first, leaders are born, then they are made.

What about you? Are you in a leadership position but not performing up to your full potential?

You do not have to settle for being an ill-equipped leader.

TEAMWORK

I saw the most interesting poster inscribed with this: "Teamwork: Many Hands, Many Minds, One Goal." I thought it was quite powerful. Here's why:

- **Many Hands**—people who are willing and capable
- **Many Minds**—people who are valued and invited to give their input
- **One Goal**—mutually agreed upon and headed in the same direction

Isn't that the essence of teamwork? The signature of best teams is in the outcomes they produce. In your role as leader, getting individuals to work well together is not just a plus, it is a must. Building effective teams is a hallmark of a leader who leads. It's the only way to achieve uncommon results.

GOOD INTENTIONS

Have you ever made plans but didn't follow through? You had good intentions, but they didn't materialize and become reality? Well, just the other day I put myself in that same situation. I had my day all planned out, but I only completed a few things on my list.

I let distractions get in my way.

I was tempted to beat myself up or worse, blame it on someone else. But that would have been futile. Then I was reminded of a quote I saw in a church bulletin which read: "Good intentions, like crying babies, should be carried out immediately." I like that! (Smile!)

Nothing against crying babies, but I immediately got the point. The next time I am tempted to take a detour, I will heed this advice. I hope you will too!

Doing so will lead to your intended destination.

KEEPING SCORE

I would not refer to myself as an avid sports fan, but as a cheerleader in high school, I learned quite a bit about sports. (And I do enjoy watching a good game every now and then.) Regardless of the sport, there is one thing I've noticed: They don't wait until the end of the game to keep score.

There is actually a person designated to record the score *during* the game.

Why? Because each team and team member need to know where they stand. Having access to this information helps them know what they are doing well and what they need to adjust in order to "best" the competition.

Although this is clearly understood in sports, why do we wait until the end of the year to give feedback on performance at work?

Twelve months is a *very* long time to wait to have a conversation with your direct reports about their performance. Quite frankly, most of us can barely remember what we did last week without referring to our notes. (Okay, perhaps that applies mostly to me. SMILE!)

"There's a right time for everything," as the Bible says. Now is the right time to review performance and give feedback to your direct reports.

Don't have any direct reports? Now is an opportune time to capture your "score." Doing so now will make it much easier when review time comes around. By the way, please don't forget to discuss this with your boss. You really need to know if they agree with your assessment. At performance review time, you'll be very glad you did.

It could make a huge difference when it comes to getting your next raise.

LEAD, FOLLOW, OR GET OUT OF THE WAY

I had the privilege of speaking at the Tennessee SHRM State Conference. There I met human resource professionals from across the state and beyond who are making a difference in their respective organizations. They must be! Their theme was: "Lead, Follow, or Get Out of the Way."

Not only did I get a chance to hear some awesome speakers, I also led a session on how to leverage managing and measuring work to move the needle on employee engagement. It is a proven fact that leaders who succeed in mastering this competency can achieve uncommon results. They do it by setting clear goals and objectives, monitoring and measuring results, and giving timely feedback.

"Lead, follow, or get out of the way" is a clarion call to us all. Which will you choose: lead, follow or get out of the way?

Please say lead.

CREDIBLE LEADERS

Credible leaders are simply . . . incredible! If you've had the privilege of working for someone who is credible, you know it. Thankfully, I have! I consider myself very fortunate to have worked for some inspiring leaders during my career. Two of my former bosses, Bruce and Don, proved to be true leaders who lead.

Dictionary.com defines *credibility* as "having the quality of being believable or worthy of trust." Synonyms include *trustworthiness, dependability,* and *integrity.*

There can be no doubt that leaders make an indelible imprint in the lives of those they lead—either positive or negative. Those who make a positive difference possess the Three Cs:
- Competence
- Composure
- Character

Leaders with these traits achieve extraordinary results.

CONFLICT RESOLUTION: "DROP THE ROCK"

The first step in resolving unhealthy conflict requires someone to "drop the rock." To "drop the rock" means that at least one party in a conflict stops fighting the other person and is willing to press for what Stephen Covey calls a "win/win."

Some would call it taking the high road. I call it taking the road that leads out of a messy situation and using precious energy to produce a better outcome. Rather than fighting the other person over who is right, take steps to do what is right—for yourself and for all parties involved.

Resolving unhealthy conflict requires being assertive and cooperative; it's sharing your thoughts and ideas *and* listening to the other person's thoughts and ideas, even when you disagree.

It may take two to tango, but it only takes one to "drop the rock."

CULTURAL COMPETENCE

While preparing for a discussion on Diversity, Equity, and Inclusion (DEI), I came across a wonderful definition of cultural competence. It is definitely one of the best I've seen and reads like this: "the ability to understand, appreciate and interact with people from cultures or belief systems different from one's own" (from apa.org).

I like the threefold nature of the definition, which signifies to me that it is progressive and develops along a continuum:

- Understand—This is consistent with one of Covey's *7 Habits of Highly Effective People*: Seek first to understand then to be understood.
- Appreciate—This is foundational to treating others with dignity and respect. It is possible to value people for who they are even when we don't like or agree with what they do.
- Interact with—To succeed in any endeavor, working well together is not just a plus . . . it's a must.

Bottom line, cultural competence is possessing the capacity to interact effectively with people from backgrounds and beliefs different than our own. It requires both skill *and* will.

I'M RIGHT... YOU'RE WRONG!

The other day I was talking with someone who made a statement I knew was factually incorrect. I tried to gently correct them, but they insisted that they were right.

I had stumbled upon one of those people who has a very strong need to be right. You know, one with a win/lose paradigm. Nothing I could say, no matter how I said it, could convince them otherwise. So I stopped trying. I heeded the advice of one of my mentors who often said, "Gwen, pick your battles."

This was a battle I chose not to fight. It was not worth the time and energy. Plus, knowing I was right was good enough. I didn't have to prove to them they were wrong. The best way to handle that particular situation was to give up my need to prove I was right.

What about you? Do you have the need to be right? No one likes to be wrong. But no one has to prove they are right all the time, either.

FOUR TYPES OF PEOPLE

The other day I listened to a talk by Robert Kiyosaki. He described four types of people:
- Those who have to be right
- Those who want to be liked
- Those who want to be comfortable
- Those who want to win

I imagine you've come across one or more of these types, and you may even be able to put a name with a face. If we're honest with ourselves, we all like to be right. (I know I do.) But I don't (and can't) know everything, so I'm not always right.

My natural personality is that I like to be liked. At times, this may result in me shying away from difficult conversations and avoiding conflict. But I must accept the fact that it's not possible (nor practical) to be liked by everyone.

And by all means, being comfortable often makes me feel safe and secure. But even that can be an illusion. Ever heard the story about the frog? Put him in boiling water, and he will jump out pretty quickly. But put him in warm water and slowly bring it to a boil, and it will get him every time.

No one in their right mind wants to lose. Everyone likes to win. But winning by any means necessary leaves you with a huge deficit, especially in the long run.

So, what about you? Which of the above best describes you?

MADE FOR MORE

For those with a traditional work schedule, it's the middle of the workweek: Wednesday (AKA Hump Day). By this time, some are thinking, *If I can just make it through Wednesday, surely I can make it to Friday. And then I can enjoy the weekend!* In effect, five days are spent . . . not invested in doing something meaningful to them.

If this describes how you experience your workweek, perhaps you're miscast. Perhaps . . . just perhaps . . . you were made for more. Perhaps there is a way to add more life to your days and more years to your life. And perhaps . . . just perhaps . . . if you look for it, you could find out what "it" is.

Wouldn't it be grand to enjoy what you do so much that it doesn't feel like work? I believe that's very possible. And it may not mean "seeking new landscapes, but only require that you have new eyes," as Marcel Proust said.

Perhaps today could be the day that, indeed, you were made for so much more.

Refuse to settle for being less than your very best.

QUITTERS

"Some employees quit and leave. Others quit and stay." It's not uncommon for employees to quit and leave. It is expected, and can occur for a number of reasons that are understandable. But what has become more problematic is the number of employees who quit and stay. It shows up in employee engagement survey results.

But what if your organization doesn't conduct a survey? It's still there, and it shows up as indifference, lower productivity, and low profitability. It happens for a number of reasons and must be resolved, because when left unchecked, it will only get worse.

This is where you come in. As a leader, it is incumbent upon you to find the root cause and implement a solution to the problem. Whether adapting your leadership style, better understanding your followers, managing and measuring work, or a combination thereof, it is possible to increase employee engagement.

Take steps to do so now. You will reap the benefits. Plus, you just might be glad they stayed.

THE EMPLOYEE GOLDEN RULE

There's a lot of talk about customer experience (CX), but not as much about employee experience.

Well, I found a great article in *Forbes* in which Shep Hyken discloses the secret to a great customer experience[5]: "The secret to a great customer experience is a great employee experience."

Shep starts out by saying, "What happens on the inside of the organization is felt on the outside by the customer." So true. I really like what he refers to as the Golden Rule for Employees: "Do unto employees as you want done unto customers."

I firmly believe that how we treat our employees is reflected in how our employees treat our customers. So, what would happen if we started treating our employees as internal customers?

What would be the WIIFM (What's in It for Me)? According to Shep, the following:

- Lower employee churn (Who doesn't want to keep good performers?)
- Built-in brand ambassadors (Happy employees gladly tell others.)

Here's one more: a highly engaged workforce.

My question to you is this: If you conducted a survey today, how would your employees rate their internal customer experience? Would the results show there's room for improvement?

Do you need to create a better employee experience? Here are six key factors:

- Vocabulary
- Feedback
- Recognition
- Accessibility
- Communication
- Empowerment

WARNING SIGNS

During my days in Internal Audit for Champion Paper Company, I had the opportunity to travel quite a bit to lots of places: some familiar and some tucked so far away you wouldn't even recognize the name.

It was during those travels that I became acquainted with this saying: "Red sky at night, sailors' delight. Red sky in the morning, sailors take warning." Just as the sky gives clues about pending weather conditions, leaders must be on the lookout for signs of weakening performance.

It is my experience that poor performance doesn't happen overnight. It is a process that begins with one missed deadline, then another, then another. Or there are poor quality results on a task, then another, then another, and so on.

It is so important to address performance issues when they first appear. That way, you can nip them in the bud by taking corrective action sooner rather than later. If you miss the warning signs (or wait too late), persistent poor performance will stall a career.

Or worse, it will become a career stopper!

LEAD WITH STYLE

I suppose it is tempting, if the only tool you have is a hammer, to treat everything as if it were a nail.
—Abraham Maslow

Ineffective leaders tend to use one style: *their* preferred style. Never quite getting the results they want and could get, ineffective leaders flex their muscles because they don't know how to flex their style. They have not yet learned what effective leaders already know: how to lead with style.

Highly effective leaders understand and practice situational leadership. They are able to lead with the style that is appropriate for the situation.

You can too!

SITUATIONAL LEADERSHIP

Some managers flex their muscles, but leaders don't have to. Why? Because they know how to flex their style . . . their leadership style, that is. Although they have a preferred style, these leaders realize there is no such thing as a "one size fits all." They practice the skills embodied in Situational Leadership Theory developed by Paul Hersey and Kenneth Blanchard. Also known as a Contingency Theory, this leadership model addresses two factors: the style of the leader and the readiness of the follower. It is a practical leadership model that, when practiced and perfected, can lead to very positive outcomes for both the leader and the follower.

LEADERS: BORN OR MADE?

There is an age-old debate as to whether leaders are born or made.

One commentator responded by saying, "Of course leaders are born. Then they are made!" This implies that all people are born with natural gifts and talents. But to develop to their fullest extent, our gifts and talents must be nurtured.

It is in the nurturing that we are "made." As we nurture our leadership qualities, we become more of who were created to be. And when that happens, we begin to "do" that which we were created to do: motivate people to work in unity toward common goals.

Leaders: Are they born? Or are they made?

"Of course, they are born. And then they are made!"

THIS WILL BE A BREEZE

If you've done a good job managing and measuring performance during the year, the annual review will be a breeze.

Why? Because you took the initiative to:
1. Set clear goals and objectives at the beginning of the year
2. Monitored progress against those goals during the year
3. Provided feedback in a timely manner

If you didn't have these conversations throughout the year, you're going to be in a world of hurt. And your people will be, too—especially if they are unpleasantly surprised.

But all is not lost.

No, you can't go back and make a new beginning, but you can start now and make a new ending. If you have not consistently followed through on the three steps above, come clean with your folks.

Admit it and fix it. That's what leaders do.

TRUST MUST BE BUILT

One of my better bosses was excellent at giving and receiving feedback. He did this by conducting quarterly performance reviews. Meetings were usually confirmed, and on the calendar at least a month in advance. Rarely were they rescheduled or postponed. In the event a circumstance arose that necessitated a change, he never rescheduled without confirming a new date. This indicated his commitment to:
- Ensuring expectations were communicated and understood
- Being willing to give feedback on performance
- Offering support where needed
- Being open to receiving feedback

During one of our discussions, he asked me, "On a scale of one to ten, how would you rate the level of *trust* in our working relationship?"

Now, I wasn't quite sure he really wanted my answer—because it was not a "ten." It was closer to a "six." And I told him so.

Guess what? He didn't even blink an eye. This was his reply: "What can we do to move it to a "seven"?

He really wanted us to work together to move it closer to a "ten," but he knew we couldn't leap from six to ten overnight.

That's because trust runs along a trend line. Trust has to be built. It cannot be manufactured.

YOU ASKED FOR IT!

Just recently I finished a project and was pretty happy about the results. I asked for feedback from the person overseeing the project, and guess what happened? They led with a positive comment quickly punctuated by a BUT . . . and then proceeded to list three things I could have done differently.

Now, I know I didn't do everything perfectly (they made sure I knew it), BUT I know there was more than one thing I did well. (Big SMILE!)

So, what is the moral of this story? Never ask for feedback? No. Ask for it and be prepared to take the bitter with the sweet. "Hope for the best and plan for the worst," as the saying goes.

I learned a lot from that interchange—about myself, about feedback, and about how to ask for it:

- **About Myself:** I was hoping the feedback would be balanced and the person would at least recognize the positives and the negatives.
- **About Feedback:** It can feel like the other person is being critical rather than constructive.
- **About How to Ask for It:** Be specific—ask what went well and what could be improved.

So, what is my hope for you? That you would ask for feedback on your performance. That you would listen to the positive and the negative and take action to improve. When giving feedback, make sure it's delivered in a constructive way.

At the end of the day, I am better because of what I learned from this experience.

I hope you will be too.

IT'S HALFTIME!

It's official: It's halftime! During my days as an accountant, by this time we would have closed the books for the first half of the year. We did this in order to compare actual results to what we forecasted (or budgeted). With that information we were able to assess how well we fared against expectations. There were only three options:
- Exceeded Expectations
- Met Expectations
- Did Not Meet Expectations

Just as this applies to the financial arena in the world of accounting and finance, it also applies to you. You've made it through six months of the year. (Yay!)

Your actual results during this time period exceeded, met, or did not meet expectations. Of course, the goal is: "Don't just meet expectations, exceed them."

How did your performance fare compared to expectations: both yours and your boss's expectations? How do you know?

Write it all down and discuss with your boss. (It will give you an opportunity to determine where you see "eye to eye" on your assessment and discuss any differences.)

If you have direct reports, do the same with the people reporting to you.

Make it official. It's halftime!

PAY AND PERFORMANCE

Have you had the BIG discussion yet? You know, the one when you talk to your direct reports about their performance from the prior year and tie it to their pay? Most managers have problems with this discussion for a variety of reasons.

- **Reason #1:** It is usually the first time direct reports hear an overall assessment that their performance either:

   Meets Expectations

   Exceeds Expectations

   Does Not Meet Expectations

- **Reason #2:** If your direct reports received little to no feedback on performance during the year, it may seem as though you're "making it up." This dramatically affects your credibility.
- **Reason #3:** Some managers have difficulty making the connection between pay and performance because there is little or no alignment between individual performance and corporate goals and objectives.

So, what is one to do? I have some good news: There is a way to correct it. As Maria Robinson says, "Nobody can go back and start a new beginning, but anyone can start today and make a new ending." Prepare as best you can for your current discussions *plus* determine that you will not be caught in this position again.

Make sure the goals and objectives for each member of your team are aligned with what is most important to the organization. And make it a point to discuss progress periodically throughout the performance year.

HERE COMES YOUR BIG ONE!

When we were growing up, my grandmother loved watching *Sanford and Son*. She could hardly wait to hear Fred say, "This is the big one!"

Just seeing this made me think about "the BIG one!" You know, the one when you and your boss discuss your performance from the prior year and tie it to your pay increase. Discussing pay and performance, two areas near and dear to our hearts, often evoke strong emotions. First, it's usually the first time we hear the boss rate our performance as either:

- Meets Expectations
- Exceeds Expectations
- Does Not Meet Expectations

Secondly, it may feel as though "they're making it up" or just going through the motions; especially if you received little to no feedback about your performance during the year,

Have you had "the BIG one" yet?

If not, be proactive. Prepare as best you can for this discussion. Then determine that you will not be caught in this position again.

> *""You can't go back and make a new beginning, but you can start now and make a new ending."*
> —Maria Robinson

PLEASE TELL THEM

I really hate to sound like a broken record, but I fully believe this is worth repeating: If your employees don't know how their performance stacks up against your expectations, please tell them. Why do I urge you to do so? Because if you don't tell them what you're thinking, how will they know? They really need to know:
- The good news—what they are doing well AND
- The not so good news (aka bad news)—what they need to improve.

Doing so gives them the opportunity to do more of the good and less of the bad. Although it may seem counterintuitive, research shows that giving timely and specific feedback actually INCREASES employee satisfaction.

If you don't tell them what you're thinking, how will they know?

Now, am I suggesting that you dive right in? Yes! (Big SMILE!)

Giving and receiving feedback are important to everyone's growth and development—yours and your direct reports.

TAKE TIME TO CELEBRATE!

Congratulations! It's mid-year and you're still here. That's good reason to celebrate! SMILE! As you approach this major milestone, start planning now to celebrate what you've accomplished. If you're the leader, try this (it has worked for me time and time again):

- Call your team together.
- Share what the team has accomplished to date.
- Let them know you appreciate their contribution to making it happen.
- Oh, and don't forget the treats: donuts, bagels or other goodies will do.

It doesn't have to be anything big or extravagant. A sincere "Thank You!" goes a long way! Your team will be glad you did. I believe you will too!

Remember, don't look at how far you have to go. Instead, look how far you've come. This is a surefire way to help your team get their second wind. You're going to need it for the next leg of the journey.

What if you're not the leader? Celebrate anyway!

Take time to celebrate what you've accomplished. Then get back in the saddle.

FABULOUS FRIDAY!

Congratulations! You've reached a milestone: it's Friday! You're very close to the finish line! I hope you'll take some time during your day to Review, Preview and Renew:

- **Review**—Take a look back at your week. How did you do? How effective were you? I'm sure there are things you would like to do differently (it can be easy to remember the struggles and stumbles), but don't forget to celebrate successes. And share with your team members too!
- **Preview**—Take some time to look ahead. What's on your radar for next week? Now is a very good time to begin thinking about what you'd like to accomplish and put your plan in place to make it happen.
- **Renew**—You've accomplished a lot this week! And it required you to expend a lot of effort. So please make plans to refuel over the weekend and sharpen your saw.

Make time to celebrate accomplishments, no matter how big or small. As you close out the week, run full force and finish strong. You'll be very glad you did!

SHARPEN YOUR SAW

If you're like most people who have a traditional workweek (Monday through Friday), by Wednesday, you're probably running on "half a tank." And by Friday you are so drained it seems you're running on fumes.

You promise yourself that you will stop to get refueled, but you keep trucking along, hoping you can make it to the weekend.

Now, we would NEVER drive our automobiles until they run out of gas (at least not on purpose), so why do we treat ourselves this way? Why do we allow ourselves to get so close to "E" (for empty) and ignore our inner "red light"?

If this describes you, it's time to "sharpen your saw."

You don't have to wait until the weekend. Sharpening your saw can become part of your daily routine.

Doing so could very well *add more life to your days and more days to your life.*

Please do not wait. Start today.

DRAMATICALLY INCREASE YOUR EFFECTIVENESS

Are you fighting fires you can't seem to put out? Spread so thin it seems you are about to break?

If this describes you, your productivity and effectiveness has probably declined. And it will continue to do so if the situation continues to persist.

But there is light at the end of the tunnel, and it is not a train coming back at you.

You can dramatically increase your effectiveness by developing habits that help you get more of the results you want and deserve. They are what Stephen Covey describes as the 7 Habits of Highly Effective People.

Practicing these habits on a daily basis has definitely made a positive difference in my life, as well as in the lives of so many others I know.

You can increase your effectiveness too! Making needed adjustments will go a long way to alleviate the conditions negatively affecting your productivity.

Start today! Take action to dramatically increase your effectiveness.

CANDID CONVERSATIONS

Sometimes it's not easy to say what you need to say, especially when it comes to those hot button topics. Sometimes, when you say what you need to say, the other person may not be in a space or place to listen. What then?

To be productive, candid conversations must be constructive, not destructive. First and foremost, be prepared. (Notice I didn't say "be armed," as for war.)

Covey's *7 Habits of Highly Effective People* have really helped me when I'm preparing for candid conversations:
- Begin with the end in mind: Be clear about the outcome/purpose of the conversation.
- Think win/win: What outcome will be good for all parties involved, not just for me?
- Seek first to understand, then to be understood: Be prepared to listen as well as speak up. There's a reason why we have two ears and only one mouth.

Is it time for you to have a candid conversation with someone? Doing so requires courage, compassion, and candor.

THE PINK ELEPHANT

There's an "elephant" in the room and it's PINK!

You know which elephant I'm talking about, don't you? It is that thing which is quite obvious—a problem or a difficult subject—that no one wants to talk about. So, we try to ignore it and act as if it's not really there.

Pink elephants are hot-button topics that bombard us every day and affect us regardless of where we live, work, worship, and play.

I'm sure you can think of more, but here are just a few that elicit strong emotional reactions:
- Politics
- Racism
- Sexism
- Religion
- COVID-19

Now, I like elephants, but not the pink ones! (BIG SMILE). And my natural tendency is to seek peace and harmony. But there are elephants in the room; they are multiplying and getting harder and harder to ignore. (The only way to harmony is through the herd of elephants.)

> *There is only one way to eat an elephant: A bite at a time.*
> **—Desmond Tutu**

So, what is one to do? Admit it and fix it.

Commit to having more candid conversations.

COARSE DISCOURSE

I don't know about you, but I have been troubled by the coarse discourse I see and hear, especially words spoken and written over social media. Words we would not dare say to someone's face but are emboldened to convey from behind a screen or keyboard.

Growing up as a kid I used to hear this quoted frequently: "Sticks and stones may break my bones, but words will never hurt me."

As a child it sounded fine, but as I grew up, I realized the quote is not true. What is true is this: Words, both spoken and written, have power to wound or to heal. It's all in how you use them. And I choose to use my words for good, to help, to heal, not to hurt.

Will you join me?

Let's jettison rude, disrespectful, and discourteous language from our written and spoken communication.

Together, we can help make our world a better place!

LET'S TALK

Have you decided that it's high time to talk with your colleague? To have a candid conversation about the pink elephant stifling the oxygen in the room? But what if you don't quite know how to make that happen?

These tips help me when preparing for candid conversations:
- Begin With the End in Mind—be clear about the outcome/purpose of the conversation
- Think Win/Win—what outcome will be good for all parties involved, not just for me
- Seek First to Understand, Then to Be Understood—be prepared to listen as well as speak up. There is a reason why we have two ears and only one mouth.

A tool I found very helpful is **Crucial Conversations: Tools for Talking When Stakes Are High**. I became familiar with it as I prepared to lead a group of medical directors and leaders through the material. Although I didn't know it at the time, it helped me navigate crucial conversations which needed to occur during my dad's short illness preceding his death.

Navigating a crucial conversation is like diffusing a bomb.
Touch the wrong wire and you set off an explosion of emotion.

Crucial conversations need to be had.
Make sure you are prepared to handle them.

LEADERS LISTEN

I was recently asked this question: What is the best piece of advice you can share on being an effective leader?

My response: Effective leaders listen.

All too often, many believe leaders do most of the talking. But I have come to know this:

> *Courage is what it takes to stand up and speak;*
> *courage is also what it takes to sit down and listen.*
> **— Winston Churchill**

Listening communicates that you respect and value the person and their opinion. It gives them a voice, letting them know they matter.

It conveys that one is open to being influenced, and it can be one of the best ways to influence others as well. When a person knows you value their opinion, they are inclined to listen to yours too.

Listening. It really is quite magical and has the potential to produce amazing results. It confirms that two heads really are better than one.

Try it. You just might like it!

LEADERSHIP AND LISTENING

Leaders who are new to their role often do a good job of observing and listening. Some even engage in what are called "listening tours" to better understand the needs of the organization and those who report to them.

But then . . . all of a sudden it seems as though they just stop listening. Or they're not as intentional about listening as they were at first. If this behavior persists, both parties lose out:
- The leader alienates their direct report.
- The direct report can miss out on making a valuable contribution.

In the end, it's a lose/lose proposition—all because the leader needed to develop their ability to listen.

What about you? Have you ever worked for a leader who was a poor listener?

Or perhaps you are a leader who has a difficult time listening. I was. And it caused serious problems. Thankfully, for both me and my team, I got help to become a better listener. You can too!

BE A WHOLE-BODY LISTENER

I blew it!

Right in the middle of facilitating a session on the importance of seeking first to understand then to be understood, I violated a cardinal rule of listening. While one person was sharing his point of view, I turned and started writing.

Guess what he did? He stopped talking.

Why? Because my body language communicated to him that I wasn't listening—that what he was saying was not important.

But that actually wasn't the case at all—what he was saying was very important—so much so that I wanted to make sure to write it down.

But there was no way he could know that unless I told him.

After he stopped talking, I said, "I'm listening." It was only then that he continued to share what he had to say.

So, what's the point of my story? It's so important to be a good listener, the kind educators call a whole-body listener.

I obviously have some work to do. What about you?

PRETENDERS

Can you recall a time when you were talking to someone and you thought they were listening, but they weren't?

Perhaps they were nodding or smiling or making some other gesture that you thought meant they were listening, but they weren't giving you their full attention.

They were doing what Stephen Covey calls "pretend listening." It is one of five levels of listening along his Listening Continuum. "Pretend listening" is not the same as being ignored, but it's fairly close (at least it feels that way).

Depending upon who you are talking to and how important the message is, there are several things you can do:
- Ask the person if you can have a few minutes of their time.
- If now is not a good time, arrange a more convenient time when the person will give you their full attention.
- But most of all, try not to do this to other people.

Listening is a skill that can be mastered. But it takes time and intention to become really good at giving someone your undivided attention.

PRECONCEIVED IDEAS

While leading a course from our Diversity At Work series, I landed upon the topic of preconceived ideas.

I like to make sure everyone is on the same page, and I do that by getting clear on what certain terms mean. By definition, *preconceived ideas* are "opinions formed beforehand without adequate evidence." The result? We make assumptions about people, and we don't even know them.

Preconceived ideas can be both positive and negative; but more often than not, they tend to be negative. For sure, the positive ones can get you in trouble, but negative opinions formed about people we don't even know tend to be more problematic.

> *The man who never alters his opinion is like standing water, and breeds reptiles of the mind.*
> **—William Blake**

So, let's examine the assumptions we make about others. Let's check to see if we are making decisions about people based on some preconceived ideas.

There's a pretty simple self-assessment that I perform periodically. I ask myself the following:

- How often do I make assumptions about others before getting the facts?
- How has doing this proven to be problematic both for me and the person I prejudged?
- Would I want someone to make assumptions about me without first getting all the facts?

Assumptions can be misleading. Keeping preconceived ideas in check helps me stay on the right track. It could prove helpful to you as well.

BIAS BLINDS US

Whether we recognize it or not, a huge barrier to working well together is bias.

There are two types of bias: *conscious* and *unconscious*.

Conscious biases tend to be explicit or expressed. We are aware of biased beliefs and attitudes toward others. And when we act based on our biases, we do so intentionally. When conscious bias is unaddressed in the workplace, it usually ends up in Equal Employment Opportunity Commission (EEOC) claims and settlements.

> Whether conscious or unconscious, bias blinds us to the value others bring to the table.

And then there are unconscious biases. They are implicit. By definition they are:
- Preconceived ideas or stereotypes about certain groups of people
- Formed outside of our own conscious awareness.

Although invisible to the carrier, implicit biases can definitely be felt by others. Left unchecked, they form major roadblocks to communication and productivity.

In a nutshell, biases hinder our ability to work well together because they blind us to the value others bring to the table.

Is bias hindering your team's ability to work well together? If so, are you ready to address it?

BIAS ABOUNDS

I've been doing quite a bit of work lately helping organizations dismantle the harmful effects of implicit bias.

To make any kind of headway in this area, you must first understand what it is and the ways in which implicit, or unconscious, bias rears its ugly head. (I'm sure you're very familiar with conscious biases, so let's focus exclusively on implicit or unconscious biases.)

During my research, I stumbled upon an interesting article entitled "17 Examples of Bias" that contained this statement: "To be truly biased means to lack a neutral viewpoint on a particular topic."

To be neutral means to be an impartial or unbiased person. Synonyms include, but are not limited to *objective*, *unprejudiced*, and *open-minded*.

The inability to be neutral (or objective) means we either have a positive or negative viewpoint on a particular topic. If it stopped with a particular topic, that would not necessarily pose a problem. The problem occurs when we project biases on to people. If we're not careful, it can gum up the gears and cause effective communication to grind to a halt.

For sure, we all have implicit biases; it's just something we humans develop. But we also have this amazing ability to change . . . if we truly want to.

What about you? Is implicit bias negatively effecting your interactions with others, especially those with whom you work?

DON'T BE FOOLED!

April 1st is celebrated as April Fool's Day. Also known as All Fools Day, it gets its name from the custom of playing practical jokes and then shouting, "April Fools!"

You may remember these pranks played on you as a kid growing up. I do. Most were done in fun and were funny. Some were hilarious and harmless. But some were not.

Which leads me to another topic: bias.

It may be April Fool's Day, but we are not fooled. Bias, both conscious and unconscious, is wreaking havoc in our world. And it is infecting the places where we work.

So how does it show up? As *isms*. Just to name a few:
- Racism
- Sexism
- Ageism
- Classism

Everything is funny as long as it's happening to someone else.
—Will Rogers

What are we to do? Erase them. But how? By using this three-step process: Detect, Correct, and Prevent.

We're not fooled, Isms. This April, the joke's on you!

BIAS IN HIRING

After working for almost twenty-five years in corporate America, I was caught up in a "right sizing," resulting in my job being eliminated. In reality, it was a downsizing for me, which meant I was in the market for a new position and a new company.

Although I was forty-seven years young at the time (Big BIG SMILE), I also had quite a bit of gray hair. (It's an attribute that runs in my family. I probably had my first gray hair by the time I turned twenty, and it just mushroomed from there. But I digress.)

During my job search, I encountered a peculiar situation. Upon observing my gray hair, one person said, "You may want to dye your hair so people won't think you're too old."

And I replied, "Well, what will they do when it grows back?"

I really couldn't believe my ears! It revealed a common *ism*: ageism. My competence and ability to do the job was being judged by the color of my hair. Imagine that.

Unfortunately, my experience is not an exception. In too many cases, it's the rule. In my case, it was ageism. But there are others, like racism or sexism or a host of other *isms*, rooted in bias. Whether intentional or unintentional, the results are still the same: Qualified candidates who could add value to the company are excluded, not because they can't do the job, but because a decision maker thinks they can't.

Does this sound familiar? Is it possible that some form of bias has infected your hiring process?

If you are involved in the hiring process or know someone who is, please consider looking at ways for removing bias from your company's hiring process.

JUST LISTEN . . . PLEASE LISTEN

Just the other day I was working on a project that was new territory for me, so I asked a colleague for some feedback.

Well, when she offered constructive feedback, I violated the cardinal rule of receiving feedback: I didn't listen.

Instead, I became defensive. I took her comments personally and started explaining why I did what I did. In essence, I opened my mouth and closed my ears—when I should have closed my mouth and opened my ears.

I didn't listen . . . at least, not at first.

Thankfully, I was able to settle down by telling myself she was trying to help me, not hurt me. Doing so allowed me to listen—to really hear what I needed to hear.

Boy, am I glad I did! The final product was *so* much better!

I'm so glad my colleague was patient and persistent. She cared enough to tell me not only what I wanted to hear—she told me what I needed to hear.

Feedback is a gift. Perhaps you have difficulty receiving constructive feedback. If this is the case, I encourage you to accept it as a gift, and discover the nuggets of truth packaged inside.

THE DIFFERENCE MAKER

My husband was trying to track down some information for a huge project he was working on. He determined that our local utility company was the best source for what he needed, so he reached out to several people. They directed him to some other folks, thinking surely they would know. But they didn't.

So, he tried again. And again. And again. Over a period of time, he kept asking, seeking, and knocking.

Until . . . he finally asked the right person. Boy, was she a lifesaver! A true difference maker! She made a night-and-day difference in the situation.

Taking my husband's cue of "praising in public and reprimanding in private" (he's a former Dale Carnegie instructor), I'd like to take this time to thank our difference maker:

"Ms. Summers, who you are makes a difference!"

Perhaps you know someone who fits this description. If you haven't already, take the time to let them know how much you appreciate them for their assistance.

It could make their day! And yours too! Big BIG SMILE!

"YOU'RE SO CLUTCH"

A colleague and I were building the board slate for a nonprofit organization. Quite frankly, we were having difficulty getting candidates to commit. But we kept on slugging away until most of the slots were filled.

And then my colleague snagged a BIG one!

To that, a young lady responded, "You're so clutch!"

You're so clutch? I did a double take. I had never heard this phrase, so I looked it up in Dictionary.com. And guess what it means? Here goes:

> In slang, *clutch* refers to something done (well) in a crucial situation, such as a *clutch play* in sports that pushes a team into victory. More broadly, *clutch* can characterize something as "excellent" or "effective."

Now, I'm not one to use much slang, but this one is worth adding to my repertoire! I hope you will too.

May you make your day as remarkable as you are. Then you will give folks several reasons to say this about you: "You're so clutch!" (Big BIG SMILE!)

EMERGING LEADERS

I have the pleasure of working with an amazing group of Emerging Leaders for the United States Department of the Navy! These men and women are members of the civilian workforce who aspire to assume the responsibility of a leadership role. They are willing to invest the time and energy now, as individual contributors, to prepare for a future opportunity.

What about you? Are you creating your leadership pipeline by preparing emerging leaders today?

> *Leaders create other leaders.*
> **—Tom Peters**

If so, you will have a corps of leaders prepared to answer the call. If not, you are not fulfilling your duty to create other leaders. But you can change that, starting today.

FORMATIVE AND SUMMATIVE ASSESSMENTS

Most of us are familiar with formative and summative assessments. Even if we didn't know what to call them, we experienced them in academic environments.

When a teacher (or professor) would test on information at intervals during the semester or school year, that was a formative assessment.

The final exam is a summative assessment.

I tended to get better results (and felt less stressed) in classes with formative assessments. I could gauge how well I understood the concepts being taught "along the way," and I tended to get a higher grade on the final exam. In the end, my GPA was helped not hurt.

Although this concept makes perfect sense in academic environments, some leaders have difficulty making the connection to the workplace. They aren't convinced that providing ongoing feedback to their direct reports is worth the time and effort.

But according to a survey by Accenture: "And innovation is happening . . . nearly half of our survey respondents (45 percent) report that they have shifted from annual feedback to ongoing feedback in the past five years. That's big news."

As a leader, which form of assessments do you employ with your direct reports? Formative or summative? Which would you prefer?

WHAT A DAY!

Have you ever had one of those days? You know, a day when it seems as if nothing is going quite right?

Well, today has been "one of THOSE days" for me! And it isn't even lunchtime! (Smile!)

Here's what happened: I got up in a rush to get to an early meeting. I received an unexpected call that lasted a lot longer than I had hoped. And THEN . . . as I get out of the car, I stepped in a glob of gum! Not good.

What to do? Explode? Go back home? No, I decided that I would continue on!

> *You can't go back and make a brand-new start,*
> *but you can start now and make a brand-new ending.*

I may not be able to make a new beginning, but I can start now and make it a better ending to this day.

Does any of this resonate with you? If so, BREATHE! It's free, and it can work wonders. (SMILE!)

Here's to a spectacular ending to one of THOSE days!

UNPLEASABLE BOSSES

It may seem that some bosses are simply unpleasable. If this is true for you (or someone you know), it's possible that boss could use help managing and measuring work, which includes:
- Clearly Communicating Expectations
- Setting Goals and Objectives
- Monitoring and Tracking Progress
- Providing Periodic Feedback

Neglecting any of these will cause problems, especially at annual review time.

If you're unclear about what is expected or unsure that your performance meets those expectations, now is the time to discover what your boss expects. Doing so now gives you the opportunity to correct performance issues and eliminate unpleasant surprises *before* your annual review. (By then it will be too late to make any significant adjustments.)

Be proactive! Take action now. Develop your plan and find out what your boss expects.

Or if you are the boss, help your direct reports to meet your expectations.

Communicating what you expect up front sets the stage for success. It will help minimize frustrations, both yours and theirs. It will also help you determine the standard of performance you will set for yourself and your team.

MANAGING UP

Managing up is designed to help you better understand how to meet and exceed your boss' expectations.

Now, in some circles, *managing up* has a negative connotation. Some believe it implies manipulating your boss, being a "yes" person, or being insincere.

But I would ask you to think about this from another perspective. Here's why.

All of us started off as individual contributors. And we probably thought of several things our boss could do in order to be a better boss. But focusing too much on your boss's behavior is unwise. First, we cannot change another person's behavior. Second, spending valuable energy complaining about what someone else is doing or not doing (and should be doing) is futile.

So, my advice is to focus on what you can do to perform at your best.

I recently read an interesting article by Dominique Rodgers entitled "Things to Say to Make Your Boss Love You."[6] They are:

1. "How can I help you achieve your goals?"
2. "I saw this wasn't done, so I did it.
3. "I agree . . ."
4. "I'd be happy to do that."

"How can I help you achieve your goals?" If your goals are not aligned with your boss's goals and objectives, that's a problem. If they are aligned, then helping your boss achieve his or her goals means you are also meeting your goals. And that's a good thing—what Stephen Covey calls a "win-win." So, following through on this first bit of advice for managing can help you meet or exceed both you and your boss' goals.

"I saw this wasn't done, so I did it." Think back to when you applied for your job. You probably thought about why you would be good for the position and why it was good for you; why you would enjoy working for the organization and the difference you could make.

Now that you are in the position, be proactive. Take the initiative to go above and beyond the call of duty—without being told. Bosses often love this attribute in employees.

It's true that some bosses prefer that you to "ask for permission instead of forgiveness." If this describes your boss, then let them know in advance that you see something that needs to be done and would like to take the lead by doing it.

"I agree . . ." This advice on managing up is not intended to make you appear to be a "yes" person, always nodding and giving assent to everything your boss says. But it does mean that you find points on which you can agree, even if you agree in part but not in whole. This allows you to find common ground.

Good bosses, secure in who they are, encourage employees to voice their thoughts on a given topic, even when they offer differing opinions. Good bosses know they don't know everything; it's just not possible. That's the reason why they need intelligent people like you on their team.

"I'd be happy to do that." While attending a board meeting, the chairperson asked for volunteers to work on a problem. I readily agreed to do so. Why? Because it needed to be done. I was able to use my expertise to help resolve the issue. Plus, I had the opportunity to work with fellow board members and get to know them better.

Volunteering to take on a task has its benefits. While helping the organization, I was also helping myself, sharpening my problem-solving skills and creating goodwill.

This advice is designed to help you succeed at work. One of the best ways I know to do that is by building a good working relationship with your boss.

ACKNOWLEDGMENTS

This book was a long time coming. It took a lot of support to pull it out of the funnel.

I must say it would have been so much easier to not embark upon writing this book, but in doing so, I would have cheated myself and so many others who have cheered me on to get this book done.

I definitely could not have done it without you.

Esther Richard, my sister and the one who helped me start pulling this all together. A voracious reader herself, I am so very thankful for her help.

Ernelle Sills, more than a colleague, for your guidance and oversight in managing the process to get this book completed. I imagine that sometimes it felt like herding cats. Thank you for your patience in helping to keep everything moving.

Don McLaughlin, my first boss out of college, a wonderful role model who showed me what a leader is and how a leader leads.

Bruce Patterson, my Honorary Boss for Life, for believing in me when I found it difficult to believe in myself. You opened the door for me to learn so many things and develop in so many ways, and for that I am forever grateful.

Jay Myer, unfortunately, we lost you much too soon, my friend. A great big thanks to Jay for introducing me to David at Morgan James, and to his editor Amanda Rooker.

David at Morgan James, my publisher, for your belief in me and the difference this work can make in the lives of leaders, especially emerging leaders.

Amanda Rooker, for your coaching and editorial advice on how to frame up the book and for helping shape the content flow.

Claudia Volkman, thank you for making yourself readily available to edit my book and for the very helpful suggestions. We hit off from the first email, and here we are today. Thank you for lending your expertise to this book.

Dotty Summerfield Giusti, for graciously agreeing to write the Foreword and for your example of leadership and belief in my leadership abilities.

Ricky Tucker, my husband and best friend forever, I am so very thankful to the Lord for you. You are the wind beneath my wings, my forever fan who always believes in me and wants only the best for me. I am grateful for your love and support.

Last but definitely not least, I am thankful to the Lord for leading me to such rich experiences with a variety of people and in so many places where I gleaned so many lessons. There is no way I could have done any of this without You. And I am still learning.

ABOUT THE AUTHOR

Gwendolyn J. Tucker is a trusted advisor and strategist with more than twenty years of invaluable experience gained in publicly traded companies. She has excelled in consulting with both small and medium-sized businesses as well as nonprofits. Her extensive expertise spans various critical areas, including Leadership Development, implementing merit-based pay processes, Diversity & Equity, and Inclusion, Facilitation and Training, and Change Management.

Gwendolyn embarked on her career in cost accounting within the paper manufacturing industry, a journey that ultimately led to her earning her designation of Certified Public Accountant. This early foundation in finance laid the groundwork for her successful career in corporate.

A significant milestone in Gwendolyn's career was being chosen to co-chair the Chairmen's Diversity Council, where she played a pivotal role in developing the company's Blueprint for Diversity. This pivotal experience led her to become the first Manager of Diversity & Inclusion for International Paper, showcasing her expertise in leading DEI initiatives at functional, divisional, and corporate levels.

One of Gwendolyn's core passions lies in Leadership and Talent Development. She firmly believes that the habit of promoting exceptional individual contributors to leadership roles, without the necessary support to develop their leadership skills, can hinder or even derail a promising career. Through her role as the president of RIX International, Gwendolyn is dedicated to equipping leaders with the tools and knowledge to build high-performing teams that consistently achieve exceptional results.

A true believer in community service, Gwendolyn represented her company on numerous boards during her corporate career, often serving in leadership positions. That still holds true today. Whether paid or unpaid, Gwendolyn believes in giving her best. It fulfills her life's mission of leaving each person and place better than she found them.

In her leisure, Gwendolyn loves sharing quality time with her husband and best friend forever, Ricky. They enjoy living, playing, and worshiping together. Ricky and Gwendolyn reside near Memphis, Tennessee.

APPENDIX I: RESOURCES

Leaders are lifetime learners.

Articles
"4 Things You Can Say to Make Your Boss Love You" (Dominique Rogers)
"Managing Up"
Conflict Management (From Wikipedia)
"Maslow's Hierarchy of Needs" (Very Well Mind Podcast)
"Behavior Theories"(Kurt Lewin Studies)

Books
The Road to Character by David Shields
FYI: For Your Improvement for Learners, Managers, Mentors and Feedback Givers by Michael M. Lombardo and Robert W. Eichinger
The Five Dysfunctions of a Team by Patrick Leoncini
Intrinsic Conflict Between Management and Leadership by Dr. Dean McCall
The Human Side of Enterprise by Douglas McGregor
A Theory of Human Motivation by Abraham Maslow
In Praise of the Followers by R.E. Kelley
The 7 Habits of Highly Effective People by Stephen R. Covey
Jung Typology Test by Carl Jung
Do What You Are by Paul D. Tieger, Barbara Barron, and Kelly Tieger

Emotional Intelligence by David Goodman
Leading Change by John Kotter
Who Moved My Cheese by Spencer Johnson
Everyone Communicates. Few Connect: What the Most Effective People Do Differently by John Maxwell
Multipliers by Liz Wiseman
Start with Why by Simon Synek
The First 90 Days by Michael D. Watkins

YouTube

How to Resolve Conflict in the Workplace- (USC-Price- Top Conflict Resolution Strategies for Managing Conflict)

4 Tips for Managing Conflict

Why Character, Not Career Success Is Key to a Life of Consequence

Lessons on Diversity and Inclusion with Dr. R. Roosevelt Thomas, Jr.

RSA Animate about the surprising truth about what motivates us

Maslow's Hierarchy of Needs

Ten Leadership Theories in Five Minutes with Michael Zigarelli and Kurt Lewin

Situational Leadership Overview with Dr. Paul Hersey

APPENDIX II: EXPECTATIONS AT WORK WORKSHEET

Purpose: Use this worksheet to record what is expected of you at work. This exercise will help you understand and clarify what is expected and by whom.

Explanation: When I am clear on what is expected of me, I am better positioned to know what I can to do to meet or exceed those expectations. Since expectations are written *and* unwritten, spoken *and* unspoken, it is important to uncover both—those that are apparent and those that are obscure.

Relationship	Describe What Is Expected (List the Top 5)	
Your Boss _____ Name	1. 2. 3. 4. 5.	
Your Team (Your Direct Reports) _____ Name _____ Name _____ Name _____ Name		

Expectations At Work

Relationship	Describe What Is Expected (List the Top 5)	
Your Peers		
Name		
Name		
Name		
Others (Internal & External)		
Name		
Name		
Name		

Expectations At Work (Continued)

APPENDIX III: ADDITIONAL RESOURCES

The Five Dysfunctions of a Team

Patrick Lencioni authored a very insightful book entitled *The Five Dysfunctions of a Team*.[7] If you have not read it, please do. I have summarized my understanding of the five dysfunctions and some practical application below.

Dysfunction #1: Absence of Trust

Trust is foundational to the functioning of any team. Without it, a group of individuals will not be able to work well together as a team. The lack or absence of trust occurs when insecurity and competition are at unhealthy levels within a group. Members question the motives and hidden agendas of fellow employees. When this behavior is present, group members tend to be reluctant to be their true selves.

Dysfunction #2: Fear of Conflict

When members of a group fear conflict, healthy debate does not occur and team members may not put forth differing ideas/opinions. Members are not honest or transparent, especially if speaking honestly may result in increased conflict. Those who fear conflict often have very strong opinions, but in their minds, it is easier (and safer) to remain silent, keeping their thoughts to themselves. It may be easier in the short-term but hidden and unresolved conflict has a high likelihood of resurfacing again.

Dysfunction #3: Lack of Commitment

Lack of commitment can occur for several reasons. One reason is that a member may not understand the goal of the team and their role in reaching that goal. Another reason could be that they do not agree with the goal of the team. Or they are not sure of the part they play on the team: either their acceptance by team members or their ability to meet or exceed what is expected of them.

Dysfunction #4: Avoidance of Accountability

Avoidance of accountability is the reluctance to set measurable goals, track results, and reward accordingly. Not holding oneself and fellow team members responsible for fulfilling their part (pulling their weight) is usually due to fear: fear of failing.

Dysfunction #5: Inattention to Results

Inattention to results is inevitable when the other barriers to teamwork are firmly in place. Lack of trust, mixed with fear, lack of commitment and avoidance can only produce inattention to results. Actually, all these combined can only lead to poor results. Meeting and exceeding expectations are intentional, not accidental.

Situational Leadership Theory

Situational Leadership Theory was developed by Paul Hersey and Ken Blanchard. It hinges on two dimensions: leader style and follower maturity. The premise is that effective leaders know how to adopt the appropriate style to the maturity or readiness of a person or group being led. Those who master these concepts realize a high degree of success. Paul Hersey and Ken Blanchard concluded that "the right leadership style will depend on the person or group being led."

Leadership = Task Behavior + Relationship Behavior

Task relates to telling or showing others what to do or how to do something specific. Relationship relates to supporting others.

Since leader style is a key component of this model, we will explore the four styles in more detail. They are:
- Telling or Directing
- Selling or Coaching
- Participating or Supporting
- Delegating

> *Effective leaders need to be flexible, and must adapt themselves according to the situation.*
> —Paul Hersey and Kenneth Blanchard

Style 1: Telling

Telling or directing is described as "High Task and Low Relationship." It is prescriptive in nature; the leader gives specific directions/instructions. This style is used when the follower is inexperienced or low in ability, as it relates to what is required in the situation. For instance, if a follower is responsible for completing a project or task that is relatively new and/or complex in nature, the leader should use this style. In this style, the leader provides close supervision.

Style 2: Selling

Selling helps the follower "buy in to the process." It involves coaching or guiding and is "High Task and High Relationship." The leader provides direction and supervision, but s/he also provides a healthy dose of encouragement. The leader encourages the follower to be involved, serves in the role of coach, and takes time to answer questions and explain decisions.

Style 3: Participating

Participating or supporting is "Low Task and High Relationship." The leader enters into a more collaborative role with the follower. Both parties take part in setting objectives. There is "shared decision making" which means the leader involves the follower in decision-making.

Style 4: Delegating

Delegating is just that. The follower has the freedom to determine how the task/project is to get done. This style is used when the follower is capable of delivering and confident that s/he can do so. The follower is encouraged to take as much responsibility as they can handle. Please note: Delegating does not mean "dumping" tasks you do not like or want to do.

Summary

Situational Leadership is a practical leadership model that, when practiced and perfected, can lead to very positive outcomes for the leader and follower. Because it focuses on determining the best leadership style for the situation and person(s) involved, the leader is encouraged to develop his/her ability to use a variety of styles, thus avoiding the pitfalls of a "one style fits all" approach.

I was introduced to this model more than twenty years ago. Of all the leadership theories, it is my favorite. Those who harness the power in the Situational Leadership Model will experience positive outcomes, for themselves and those they lead.

THE TOP THREE MISTAKES LEADERS MAKE AND HOW TO AVOID THEM

Time and time again leaders make some of the same mistakes when it comes to managing and measuring work. The top three are failure to:
1. Set Clear Goals and Objectives
2. Monitor and Track Progress
3. Provide Timely Feedback

All three are critical to success. Neglecting any of these will prove problematic at annual/salary review time.

Why are these so important to success?

As a leader, a major responsibility of your role is to manage and measure work, both yours and those of your direct reports. Therefore, it is incumbent on you to get well acquainted with your company's performance management processes and procedures. Once you are familiar with what is required, it is time to execute what is outlined.

Unfortunately, too many leaders fail to master the skills associated with managing and measuring the work of others. Successful leaders, leaders who lead, understand how important it is to a team's overall performance.

It is in your best interest, both in the short-term and in the long-term, to master skills related to these areas. Let's take a look at each.

Set Clear Goals and Objectives

Setting goals fuels us to go the distance.

Clear goals and objectives identify what is expected and must include metrics or key performance indicators (KPIs) that tell if or when the goal is reached. You need metrics in order to manage and measure work. Individual (and team) goals and objectives must be aligned with the organization's strategic goals and objectives.

To do this, the organization must identify its goals and communicate them in such a fashion that they are understood to everyone within the organization. If this is not common practice within your organization, there may be a lot of *activity* but it will not be *productivity*. There is a BIG difference. Productivity is productive activity; it contributes to the mission and helps to move an organization closer to achieving its mission.

Being clear on what is expected *BEFORE* the performance period begins helps set the foundation upon which solid performance can be built. This includes clarifying what your boss expects and getting it in writing. Communicating expectations up front helps both you and your team get off on the right foot, increasing the likelihood of success.

Self-Assessment:
On a scale of 1-5 (1=low, 5=high):
- How would you rate yourself in this area?
- How would your direct reports rate you in this area?

Monitor and Track Progress

The only way to fail is to stop trying to succeed.

Ideally, goals should be set by the first day of the fiscal year. (For most organizations, the fiscal year coincides with the calendar year beginning

January 1.) Doing so before the beginning of the performance year gives your direct report the full year to accomplish the goals and objectives.

Once goals have been established for each individual, the next step is to identify how you will measure what is achieved. They should include both quantitative and qualitative data which will be used to determine what progress has been made toward reaching the goal. This allows you and your direct report to discuss progress against pre-set goals aligned with the organization's strategic goals and objectives. Having objective metrics helps to eliminate subjectivity and levels the playing field.

Self-Assessment:
On a scale of 1-5 (1=Low, 5=High), how would:
You rate yourself in this area? _____
Your direct reports rate you in this area?_____

Provide Timely Feedback

"Sharing timely feedback heightens everyone's effectiveness."

Providing timely feedback is very important to managing and measuring work; and should be given in both formal and informal settings.

For example, I recommend giving impromptu feedback close to the time the person's performance is observed. If it is positive feedback, I will make my comments in the presence of others (if the employee is comfortable with me doing so).

If the feedback is constructive or corrective, I recommend sharing it with the person alone.

It is in line with one of Dale Carnegie's principles: "Praise in public. Reprimand in private."

Formally, leaders should meet one/one with each direct report at least quarterly. The purpose of the meeting is to discuss performance: what is going well and what needs to be corrected.

During the one/one is also a good time for you, the leader, to ask for feedback on how you can best support your direct report in reaching his or her goals.

Providing timely feedback allows you to discuss progress at intervals, instead of waiting until it is too late to take corrective action to reach the goal.

Self-Assessment:
On a scale of 1-5 (1=Low, 5=High), how would:
You rate yourself in this area?_____
Your direct reports rate you in this area? _____

Summary
Communicating expectations upfront and checking in periodically makes conducting the overall evaluation so much easier.

Not only does it minimize the likelihood of surprises, it serves to build trust between the leader and their direct reports.

When direct reports know what is expected, receive feedback and feel supported, conflicts can be kept to a minimum.

Steps You Can Take
When it comes to managing and measuring work, I recommend taking the following steps to avoid making these mistakes:
- Summarize Your Self-Assessment
- Set Goal to Improve
- Celebrate Your Accomplishment

Summarize Your Self-Assessment
Starting with an assessment proves helpful because it allows me to get feedback on my performance. I recommend completing a self-assessment and asking for feedback from your direct reports. Remember, this is about you improving your outcomes.

Complete the following section below.

Rate on a scale of 1-5 (1=Low, 5=High)

Action	Self-Assessment	Rated by Direct Reports
Set Clear Goals & Objectives		
Monitor & Track Progress		
Provide Timely Feedback		

Managing & Measuring Work Self-Assessment

Set Goal to Improve

Armed with feedback gathered in the Assessment, you can establish a goal to get you closer to the outcomes you most desire. I recommend setting this goal in concert with your supervisor/manager, who can provide you continuous feedback and support in achieving your goal.

Celebrate Your Accomplishment

Congratulations! If you have gotten to this point, it means you are serious about doing the work to achieve outstanding results. I celebrate you for taking the first step.

Keep up the great work!

When we work at our highest level, our performance is breathtaking.

EXAMPLES OF LEADERSHIP IN ACTION

I am fortunate to have worked for some fabulous bosses over the course of my career. And I have been in the presence of leaders I highly respect. Here are examples of some leaders I have seen in action, either as my boss or from observation. These people have modeled leadership for me. Their examples may help you better understand what leadership looks like.

DON MCLAUGHLIN

Don McLaughlin is the boss who hired me for my first "real" job. I was a recent graduate with my degree in accounting with some experience as a co-op at another paper manufacturing company, and Don was the perfect person to be my supervisor.

Although that was a *long* time ago, Don and I have stayed connected. After my departure from the company, we had many opportunities to check in with each other and see how things were going.

Needless to say, Don made an indelible imprint on my life. When I asked Don to rate his top five leadership traits, here's what he shared with me:

- Character
- Composure
- Competence
- Courage
- Care for people

I must say, I was not surprised. Over the course of the years that I have known Don, he consistently modeled these traits. These are not just words on a page; they are words he lives by. I can also say with confidence that my colleagues and those who know Don would wholeheartedly agree.

> *Being principle-driven is not about comfort;*
> *it's about doing what is right.*
> **—Donald R. McLaughlin**

One day I had an opportunity to sit down with Don to talk about leadership and how to become a better leader. I asked him what advice he would give leaders today. This was his reply:

For emerging leaders: Do the blocking and tackling very well. Being successful is coming up with good ideas, but most overlook the simple things. Have a sense of urgency, communicate, follow-up, understand the goals of the organization, and share with people on a consistent basis. If a leader does that very well, they will cover a large part of their job. Humility is a strength. It will carry you a long way. Pride never leads to success. It's not just a spiritual thing; it's an everyday thing.

For experienced leaders: First, stay up with the times. Stay abreast of changes, both in the marketplace and internal to your organization. A leader doesn't have to know how to do everything that people who report to them know how to do. Second, you still have to lay out clear expectations for people and talk about them often. Those things never change.

When I was wrapping up our conversation, Don shared these parting comments about two things he noticed during his career:

- We still have a lot of poor leaders out there.
- I am still amazed that people tend to not want to be leaders. Due to the awesome responsibility of having to do more with less, most prefer to be individual contributors.

While talking with Don, my mind was flooded with fond memories. I was reminded of how fortunate I was to have Don as my first boss out of college. He was an excellent role model then, and he still is. Little did I know how his leadership would shape who I am today.

I am very thankful to Don for making a positive difference in my life.

BRUCE PATTERSON

Bruce Patterson, whom I lovingly call my "Honorary Boss for Life," is another leader who has significantly impacted me both personally and professionally. He has served as mentor, sponsor, and friend.

He became vice president of the Internal Audit Department about five years into my career. Bruce shared insights on some of the most challenging and most rewarding things about being a leader.

Who is the leader who has influenced you the most?

That's a hard question to answer; 90 percent of my leaders have influenced me in a positive way. But if I had to name one, it would be Austin Moore. The most important lesson he taught me was how to delegate. He was a key influencer who helped me focus and develop.

You develop as you delegate. Not only do you develop your ability to trust others, but the person to whom you delegate gets the opportunity to grow their skills too.

You only have so much time to do things. If I tried to do everything, I wouldn't have time to develop. Delegating gave me the opportunity to continue to grow and develop.

Delegating meaningful assignments lets your people know you trust them.

How did Austin's influence shape your leadership style?

In addition to learning how to delegate, Austin taught me to ask, "What's the real problem?"—to focus on finding the right answer for the situation, not what is going to make me look successful.

Because I don't have a huge ego, it's easy for my response to be, "What's the right answer in the situation?" Then, when I figure out what is right (without regard to how it will make me look), I can figure out how to execute.

Understand what the issue is. Then focus on how to fix it. With Austin's tutelage, I was able to move out of just being an accountant. I developed my ability to understand the business and apply that knowledge to add value to the organization.

> *Give credit where credit is due. Let your people be the star of the show.*
> —Bruce Patterson

What has been the most challenging about being a leader?

I believe people are inherently good. Therefore, it's not hard for me to look for the best in people. I don't let style affect my trust in a person.

Because of that, one of the most challenging things is trusting people, then finding out they are distrustful. Assuming people are doing something for the right reason—only to find out that they aren't.

For example, doing a sensitive investigation into a situation and realizing the people are not good.

I tend to bend over backward to make sure folks are successful. In hindsight, I may have waited too long to deal with an issue. But eventually you have to deal with it, and sometimes sooner rather than later.

Another challenge is when people won't listen to you, even when you have their best interests at heart.

What has been the most rewarding about being a leader?

The most rewarding thing is getting feedback that I helped in some way. In particular, I had a manager who was having difficulty with interpersonal communication, but she was open to feedback, and I saw her blossom. It's also rewarding:

- When people seek feedback and they take it for the right reason.
- When I feel I've made a positive difference in a person's life.

> *Don't make assumptions. Doing so will get you in trouble.*
> — Bruce J. Patterson

What advice would you give to emerging and experienced leaders?

You have to be very open; seek feedback and give feedback. Without feedback, no one is a successful leader. When giving feedback, you must give it in the appropriate way. Be willing to adjust your style.

Ask your people for their opinions and be open to listening. Allow discussion. The focus must be on getting to the right answer.

As a leader, it is imperative that you help your people help you. Some leaders worry about how they are going to look. It should be about what is right. When your team looks good, you look good. You're part of the team. Utilize all the talents you have on the team to do what's right for the organization.

Bottom line: Support your people. Respect them. Thank them. It's inexpensive. It's so easy. But we are often reluctant to do it.

I start with the belief that if you hire good people, they want to do the right thing, but sometimes they just don't know how. So my goal is to help them do the right thing.

Bruce's Top 5 Traits of a Leader

1. Make sure you want to get to the right answer.
2. Get and give feedback.
3. Be a delegator.
4. Be honest and transparent.
5. Be empathetic of the person and the situation at hand. Make sure you don't leave dead bodies lying around.

To find Bruce's Quotable Quotes and Bio, scan the QR Code located in the front of this book.

I had the privilege of working with Bruce for eight years. Under his leadership, I grew both personally and professionally. Bruce Patterson's comments on leadership are more than words. Bruce not only talks the talk, he "walks" the talk. I am very thankful that he made an indelible imprint in my life, bringing out the best in me. Once while at a crossroads in my career, I reached out to Bruce for advice. I kept saying I wanted to make the RIGHT decision. Thinking I had to make the RIGHT decision stirred up fear that I would make the wrong decision. And Bruce said, "Gwen, just make the best decision with the information you have. Just that simple statement seemed to relieve the pressure.

> *Get the right input from the right people so you can make the best decision.*
> **— Bruce Patterson**

RICKY L. TUCKER

Although I have known Ricky Tucker for almost eighteen years, I get to know him up close and personal each and every day.

In case you have not noticed, we have the same last name. No, we are not siblings. He is my husband. And often living what you teach is often hardest with those you love. But that is definitely not the case with Ricky. That's why it was very important for me to capture his comments on leadership and share them with you.

Ricky has an extensive career in a variety of companies and leadership positions. From Verizon to Maryville College to founding his own executive coaching firm, RIX International, LLC, Ricky is purposeful about showing people how to be their very best.

Below are some insights into how he became the leader he is today.

> *Remember to always be your best!*
> —Ricky Tucker

Who has had the most influence on you as a leader?

Apart from my mom, I would say that three people come to mind. They each had a significant impact on me professionally and as a leader:

1. **Mr. Taylor**, my Distributive Education teacher at East High School, had faith in me. He selected me to participate in a State Level sales competition. He celebrated my accomplishments.
2. **Mr. Blasingame** promoted me to sales manager over ten other sales reps who had more tenure in the company. He encouraged me to continue the path I was on and gave me an opportunity because he realized I was committed, worked hard, had discipline, and was a team player. That promotion led to another opportunity to be hired at the corporate level. Having prior management experience positioned me for promotions.

3. **Dan** was an awesome leader. Under his leadership, I was selected to fill multiple leadership roles. Because he knew I was coachable, hardworking, and committed to working as a team member, I secured my largest roles with the greatest responsibility of my career.

What has been the most challenging about being a leader?

Managing and leading individuals who don't have a similar drive, discipline, or desire to improve. Leading a diverse group of people with different personalities and work styles, and bring them together to successfully work as one can definitely be challenging. Fortunately, the majority of the people I have worked with trusted and respected me. As a result, I've experienced few problems as a leader.

What advice would you give to emerging/aspiring and experienced leaders today?

My advice to both would be the same:
1. Treat people the way you would want to be treated, whether the situation is easy or complex.
2. Pay attention to details.
3. Be empathetic.

Ricky's Top 5 Traits of a Leader
1. Respect
2. Integrity
3. Excellence
4. Listening
5. Effective Communicator (verbal and written)

Top Picks: Leadership Books and Tools
- *The 7 Habits of Highly Effective People* by Stephen R. Covey
- *How to Win Friends and Influence People* by Dale Carnegie

- *Let's Get Results, Not Excuses* by James M. Bleech and Dr. David G. Mutchler

Quotable Quotes
- "Remember to always be your best!"
- "People don't care how much you know until they know how much you care."
- "Lead by example."
- "Be ready so you don't have to get ready."

As you can see, I am very fortunate that I get the benefit of sharing life with my husband, who has a love for leadership and for helping emerging leaders discover the leader within.

TIMOTHY FLORENCE

Timothy Florence provides insight into how an authentic leader leads. I had the chance to work with Timothy and his team while I was leading training for University Clinical Health at UTHSC. As director of Instructional Services Technology at the University of Tennessee, Timothy and his team were responsible for handling IT support. Over and over again, he and his team exceeded my expectation.

One day, I had an opportunity to extend my gratitude to Timothy. He gave all the credit to his team. To which I responded, "What's in the leader shows up in the people!"

It was then that I knew I had to sit down with Timothy to get insights on how he and his team deliver excellent customer service over and over again.

How would you define leadership?

Leadership to me is encouraging and inciting others through word and deed to accomplish common goals.

As it relates to leadership, who has impacted you the most?

First and foremost would be the Christ found in the Scriptures who set the perfect example of leadership. One can learn a lot from reading how he lovingly dealt with imperfect humans.

Mr. Steve Butler and Dr. Ken Brown are not only close friends but are strong examples of leadership. They have had a significant impact on how I view leadership. I've watched them lead by example for many years. I'm also privileged to report to Vikki Massey (Deputy CIO) and Dan Harder (CIO). They have proven to be a good support system for our team.

What are three ingredients for getting your team to work well together?
1. Respect
2. Empathy
3. Love

There must be a certain level of respect among people that work together. Empathy is also a key ingredient because as we know, things happen. I try to show the team how to be understanding and empathetic when other team members "appear" to fall short, giving them the benefit of the doubt as we would want others to give us during difficult times. The last ingredient, love, is the most important because it is the common glue that connects all other altruistic qualities. Genuine love for people makes all good things possible. Any initiative will likely fail without it.

Please share your insights on what it means to be customer-focused.

Being customer-focused starts from within. It stems from an internal desire to please others. Those who have a real interest in helping people are willing to put others before themselves and will exhaust all possibilities to be of assistance. Such an innate desire is not driven by money— although monetary rewards are always appreciated. However, serving others out of coercion or from another motive typically does not hold up when things get difficult. Rather, it is the deep satisfaction one receives from aiding someone in need. Such a person does not need prodding and will be customer-focused regardless of the customer.

As a leader, what are the top challenges you face?

The most significant challenge is leading a team of people with various personalities and backgrounds to achieve a common goal. Age, background, knowledge, experience, frames of reference, and personalities all vary among team members. To successfully lead such a group often requires patience and a little creativity.

Another challenge is resources. Resources are usually always limited regardless of the nature of the work. This too takes creativity as we strive to improvise and make the most of what we have. Teamwork, cohesiveness, and good planning also help to mitigate such issues.

Please share insights on your leadership philosophy.

First, it is not about me. We often hear the phrase "there is no I in team." While this is true, a successful leader must exhibit sincere humility and selflessness. Such a trait is easily seen in everything one says and does. Humility is often contagious and has a greater impact than words that may be spoken in a team meeting.

There are various forms when it comes to leadership. The Chameleon Style has several advantages as it allows leaders to be flexible. To live by one form of leadership may not as effective. Circumstances, environment, team characteristics, uncontrollable events, and other constantly changing variables can have a direct correlation as to be the best style of leadership.

One form of leadership to which I am partial is the Servant Style. A leader can find the servant philosophy useful if he or she is leading a team of dependable, self-starting members. Employees are most productive when they are happy and can see the impact of their contributions. My goal is to make sure they have what they need and get in the trenches with them when they need my assistance.

In parting, are there any leadership resources you recommend?

There are two textbooks that provide great theoretical insights on leadership. The first is *Leadership: Theory and Practice* by Peter G. Northouse which gives a good, in-depth overview of the various forms of leadership.

Work Motivation: History, Theory Research, and Practice by Gary P. Latham is another reference that gives practical guidance, in addition to theory of how to engage teams.

Timothy's Quotable Quotes

- "Your greatest asset is people."
- "A successful leader must exhibit sincere humility and selflessness."
- "There must be a certain level of respect among people that work together."

JIM DUNCAN

Jim Duncan gives a bird's eye view into what has made him a successful leader. A leadership and management consultant, Jim is a retired executive director of the Memphis Botanic Gardens and former division president of Smith and Nephew.

I had the privilege of hearing Jim speak on Transformational Change at the Alliance for Nonprofit Excellence Annual Conference. (It was there that I first heard his famous Mustard Story, a fascinating story on the importance of giving corrective feedback in a constructive manner. It is quite insightful.)

For *The Mustard Story*, its message, and its meaning, check out the full story here: www.leaderwholeads.com/the-mustard-story.html.

Jim's Quotable Quotes

- "Leaders must lose the 'one size fits all' mentality."
- "The quickest route to a leader's demise is the 'I know it all' mentality."
- "Effective leaders speak and think in terms of *we* and not me."

PAUL RECORDS

I am very fortunate to have reported to and/or worked with some incredible leaders during my career. Paul Records is one of those people, a credible leader. I consider him a mentor and had a chance to work with him during my days at Champion Paper Company when he was Senior Vice-President of Human Resources.

During my interview with Paul, I was intrigued by his insights on leadership and mentorship. This is how he defined the two: *Leadership* is about influencing organizations and individuals, setting a vision, empowering employees, and helping people get to a place. *Mentorship* is when two individuals engage in a mutually rewarding relationship through which both parties learn and grow personally and professionally.

During the course of my career, I came to realize that leaders, mentors, and sponsors all played integral parts in my development as a leader.

Are mentors and sponsors similar or essentially different? How do you differentiate between the two?

There are elements of similarity, yet strong differences. I refer to *sponsorship* as "the invisible hand." Sponsors create opportunities that test abilities and reward good performance. In many cases, you might not know your sponsors. They are people who are invested in your success, but often you have no clue of the role they play.

On the other hand, *mentors* are well positioned to help people understand the unwritten rules, how things really work. They help you understand today and tomorrow as well.

A sponsor's task or focus is to get you to participate in something outside of your normal technical skill set. Sponsorship is similar to "air cover" in the event issues surface. They invest in you, speak for you, and believe in you. When issues surface, they deflect heat to give you breathing room to get things back on track.

Paul's Quotable Quotes
- "Insights and perspectives are best shared when an individual is receptive."
- "If it's worth doing, do it right and understand why doing it right matters."
- "I believe the most important skill for a leader is listening to really understand what is happening and put forth a solution."

To read more about Paul and the insights he shared, please do so here: www.leaderwholeads.com/paul-records-on-mentorship.html and www.leaderwholeads.com/paul-records-on-leadership.html.

LEADERSHIP AND PERSONALITY STYLES

Leadership and Personality Styles focuses on helping leaders understand how their style affects their ability to be effective in their role. My favorite assessment is the Jung Typology, developed by Carl Jung and Isabella Briggs-Myers. If you have never taken this assessment, please consider doing so now.

A Note of Caution

As a note of caution: The purpose of this assessment is not intended for the purpose of labeling you or others. It is a springboard to understanding yourself and others.

And, indeed, understanding is a beautiful thing—especially when you are charged with leading a group of individuals who must learn to work as a team.

Background

Once you complete the Jung Typology, you will receive a "Four Letter" type formula representing four dimensions:
- Extroversion (E)
- Sensing (S)
- Thinking (T)
- Introversion (I)
- Judging (J)
- Intuition (N)
- Feeling (F)

- Perceiving (P)

These run along a continuum. Neither one is good or bad, which is why each can range in value from 0 to 100 (representing degrees to which you are either one or the other). For example, my type is ENFJ, which means I have a preference toward Extroversion, Intuition, Feeling, and Judging.

The Four Dimensions

Extraversion and Introversion

Prior to conducting much research on personality styles, I described an extrovert as outgoing and introvert as less so, or shy. In this case, however, extraversion and introversion simply describes the source from which one draws their energy: by being with others or retreating within to quietness and peace.

Sensing and Intuition

This dimension describes how one takes in information. For the person who is sensing, s/he relies more heavily on what s/he can take in through the five senses. They tend to focus on what is practical, has a high respect for what is and what works. The person described as intuitive has a tendency to speak in terms of possibilities, imagining what could be.

Thinking and Feeling

This dimension refers to how a person processes information. Those described as "thinking" tend to be described as rational, cool and reserved, whereas those who are "feeling" tend to be warm and readable. As it relates to conflict, "thinking" types tend to be invigorated by it, while those who are "feeling" types tend to resist it.

Judging and Perceiving

This dimension speaks to how a person makes decisions and how much information is needed before a decision will be made. Those with the tendency for Judging makes decisions rather quickly. The person described as "Perceiving" often likes to explore the options and may be slow to make a decision. Leadership and personality styles can "clash" in this area, especially if the leader and follower differ significantly in how they make decisions.

A WORD TO WOMEN WHO LEAD

Since I am a woman who leads, I wanted to share a special word with you. It contains insights gained from my own experience, as well as wisdom gleaned from those who served as mentors and sponsors along the way. I am convinced that, regardless of where you are on your leadership journey, you will find information to help you grow and become a better leader who leads.

I am very fortunate to have had some very positive experiences in my career. Starting in cost accounting, all of my corporate experience was in Fortune 500 manufacturing environments. My leadership training was largely in predominately male environments until I had the privilege of completing the Smith College Consortium on Strategic Thinking.

At Smith College I had the opportunity to collaborate with a group of dynamic women from other Fortune 500 companies who served in leadership positions at all levels within their organizations. That's where I experienced the power of what happens when women come together. And I would like to recreate that experience for other women who lead.

It was there that these words, penned by Marianne Williamson, were etched in my memory:

We ask ourselves, "Who am I to be brilliant, gorgeous, talented, fabulous?
Actually, who are you not to be?

What I experienced at this training is very hard to put into words, but I do know this: I was forever changed. Since that time, I have been on a mission to be the leader I was born to be. And to help others do so too.

The ABCs

We all have to start from somewhere, so let's start with the ABCs:
- Be Authentic
- Be Bold
- Be Credible

In the sections below, I share how the ABCs above have manifested as I have developed as a leader.

Be Authentic

Most of us are familiar with the statement "Be like Mike." It originated from a Gatorade commercial with Michael Jordan as the star.

It's OK to be like Mike—if your name is Mike. But if not, "Be yourself" is so much better. This wise advice was given to me by Karen, a colleague and friend.

Each of us is an original, like no one else. Unique, valuable, and possessing our own genius. Those are the very attributes that qualified you for your position of leadership.

To discover your uniqueness and genius, please take a few minutes to complete your personality profile by scanning the QR Code at the front of the book. Knowing my personality style gave me a deeper insight into my own personality and helped me better leverage my strengths in my leadership position. I believe it can do the same for you.

> *What lies beyond us and what lies before us are tiny matters when compared to what lies within us.*
> **—Ralph Waldo Emerson**

Be Bold

Another part of Marianne Williamson's poem reads like this:

> *Our deepest fear is not that we are inadequate.*
> *Our deepest fear is that we are powerful beyond measure.*
> *It is our light, not our darkness that most frightens us.*

Women who lead are not in the habit of playing it safe. We don't throw caution to the wind, but we do take calculated risks that leads to desired outcomes.

Being bold means pressing beyond the borders of our comfort zones in order to achieve uncommon results. This is the "stuff" the most effective leaders are made of. At times being bold means standing alone. It means having the courage to move forward, even in the presence of fear. Women who lead are not afraid to stand alone.

I had the pleasure of being in the room with Scott Hamilton, an Olympic Figure Skating Gold Medalist for the USA. I love his definition of courage. He says that "courage is fear that has said it's prayers."

Be Credible

There can be no doubt that leaders make an indelible imprint in the lives of those they lead, either a positive one or a negative one. Women who lead make a positive difference because they possess the 3 Cs of Credibility:

- Competence
- Character
- Composure

Women who lead know that credibility is built over a lifetime but can be lost in a moment . . . in the blink of an eye. That is why we take great care to preserve our credibility by preparing to lead, preparing our team, and preparing to succeed.

Women who lead succeed when they possess the ABCs in increasing measure. A woman who leads is powerful—a force to be reckoned with—and produces uncommon results.

Yes, that sounds just like you!

If you should ask yourself, "Who am I to be brilliant, gorgeous, talented, fabulous? This is my reply: "Actually, who are you not to be?"

Needless to say, my experience at Smith College was life-changing. I left there better than when I came. That is my desire for you, too—that you will leave this place better than when you came.

TOP CHALLENGES WOMEN FACE

Women are strong and are known for being high achievers. Often taken for granted in the workplace, more and more responsibility is being placed on women who are ready to step up to the plate.

Even with a great track record and being known as the go-to or subject matter experts, women face a number of challenges, in both in leadership and in life.

Let's take a look at the top challenges women face in the workplace that directly impact their personal financial bottom line. In other words, their purchasing/buying power and ability to build wealth. The top three challenges I am referring to are:
- Underpaid
- Underrated
- Underestimated

Let's take a deeper look into possible reasons why these challenges exist.

Underpaid

The gender pay gap is real. It's the number-one challenge women face in the workplace.

Data from a 2022 survey on women and pay shows that women earn 82 percent, on average, of what men earn. Female managers fare a bit better; they earn 90 percent.

When you dig deeper, there is some explanation as to why there is a pay gap. The terms, as defined by the Women's Foundation, are:
- Uncontrolled Gender Gap—measures median salary for all men and women regardless of job type, seniority, location, industry, years of experience, etc.
- Controlled Gender Gap—measures pay for men and women with the same job and qualifications.
- Pay Scale—the controlled gender pay gap tells us what women earn compared to men when all compensable factors are accounted for, such as job title, education, experience, industry, job level, and hours worked.

Underrated

During my career in corporate America, annual performance reviews were mandatory. As an individual contributor, I had periodic conversations (usually quarterly) with my direct supervisor about my performance.

When I moved into a leadership position, not only did I have discussions about my performance, but it was expected that I would have review performance results with my direct reports. The purpose was to give and get timely feedback on goals and objectives set at the beginning of the performance period.

Therefore, you can imagine how aghast I am when women tell me they have infrequent discussions about their performance. Some report having an annual discussion, while others say they have **none at all**.

Not having stated goals and objectives at the beginning of the performance period AND infrequent discussions on performance is a surefire way to be underrated.

To prevent being underrated, make sure you are:
- Clear on goals and objectives up front
- Check in periodically to ensure you're on track
- Communicate overall results at end of performance period

Let's be clear on why we're here.

Underestimated

To be underestimated is to be perceived as less capable, as someone who does not measure up and doesn't have what it takes to get the job done.

It's not a foreign concept for women because it has been an age-old challenge and opportunity for women in the workplace to overcome.

I thought it was interesting that Pay Scale states that "the controlled pay gap tells us what women earn compared to men when all compensable factors are accounted for—such as job title, education, experience, industry, job level, and hours worked," but says nothing about performance or about how women add value to the company's bottom line compared to men.

What about you? If you are a woman who leads in the workplace, are you facing any of these challenges?

I believe hidden within every challenge there is at least one opportunity. In the challenges you face, could there be an opportunity to take action that gets you what you want most?

What if:

- Instead of underpaid, you could close your pay gap.
- Instead of underrated, you could set yourself up for success.
- Instead of underestimated, you could show proof of how you add value.

PARADIGMS OF HUMAN INTERACTION

A paradigm is a frame of reference or theory that affects how we see and experience a situation. By definition, it represents a "group of ideas about how something should be done . . . or thought about." Stephen R. Covey identified six paradigms of human interaction. They are:
- Win/Win
- Win/Lose
- Lose/Win
- Lose/Lose
- Win
- Win/Win or No Deal

Win/Win

> *Win/Win is a frame of mind and heart that constantly seeks mutual benefit in all human interactions.*
> —Stephen Covey

Although there is an appropriate time to use each paradigm, Win/Win is the preferable approach for those who must work together to achieve maximum results. Win/Win is a mindset or approach to a situation that seeks to ensure the interest of all parties are considered. It is not an "either/or" proposition. Covey describes Win/Win as "not your way or my way; it's a better way, a higher way." And it leads to what Covey calls the "Third Alternative."

The person who practices this paradigm is principle-centered, places emphasis on what is right/best for *all* parties involved and is not focused on getting the upper hand or the best deal for themselves.

Win/Lose

Win/Lose is where one party asserts their interests over the interests of another. They subscribe to the "scarcity mentality" and believe "you must lose so that I can win." This interaction often feels highly competitive in nature and destroys teamwork.

Lose/Win

Lose/Win means I cooperate with the other person to the degree that I lose so they can win. In this approach, the "loser" often walks away very resentful. More often than not, this person chooses to lose in order to avoid conflict.

Lose/Lose

Lose/Lose is when no one wins; both parties lose and both end up with very hard feelings. This approach does not serve to advance positive team dynamics and is very unhealthy for all parties involved.

Win

The person operating with this paradigm says, "I want to win. I don't want you to lose, but getting what you want is your business, not mine." They do not actively seek to ensure that the interests of the other party are considered.

Win/Win or No Deal

The Win/Win or No Deal mindset actively seeks the interests of all parties involved, including theirs. It requires a high character ethic, investment of time, and lots of two-way communication.

In the event an agreement suitable to all parties cannot be reached, the only Win/Win is No Deal. Even if no deal is the best outcome, the intent and engagement of this interaction sets the stage for possible Win/Wins in the future.

Summary

As long as you seek Win/Win in your interactions, it really does not matter which paradigm the other party has. Of course, this will require strong communication, negotiation, and conflict management skills, but the person with the skills to obtain Win/Win outcomes will prevail.

LEADERSHIP AND TRUST

Trust is the glue of relationships.
—Stephen R. Covey

One of the best things you can give your people is a reason to trust you.

In discussing trust, let's define some terms. Webster's Dictionary defines trust as "firm reliance in the honesty, dependability, strength or character of someone." Hyler Bracey builds on Webster's definition to create a working definition of trust:

> Trust is my faith in your ability or word in some specific area. Faith means I believe that you are capable of doing what you say you can do and that you will actually do it if you say you will. Trust includes the degree to which I believe you will look out for my best interest in a specific area. Trust can rise or fall depending on the person and the situation.
>
> Part of a trusting relationship goes beyond believing you are capable and true to your word. It also suggests that you care about my welfare and success in helping me achieve my goals.[8]

Trust is never given to another person globally and unconditionally. It always has to do with a specific area of expertise or action. Trust involves both ability and word. You are capable in this area and true to your word if you promise to do something in that area. Trust comes in different degrees or levels, even as it is always defined relative to some area of action or behavior.

Though trust can be one-sided, it is best when it is mutual. Trust can grow between people, or it can erode. Lost trust can also be recovered and rehabilitated. Trust can be built. There are methods and skills for facilitating it.

> *Trust runs along a trend line.*
> *It has to be built; it cannot be manufactured.*
> —Hyler Bracey

> *Trust is the willingness to be vulnerable to the actions of another.*
> —R. C. Mayer

Praise for Building Trust

I had the privilege of leading a group of leaders through Hyler Bracey's book *Building Trust*, which examines principles that are foundational to building trust in relationships. This book offers practical ways to apply the concepts in real-work situations, including giving and receiving feedback.

It's a must-read and one of my top picks. If this book is not in your collection/library, I encourage you to add it today.

LEVELS OF LISTENING

Stephen R. Covey's Listening Continuum identifies five levels of listening:

Listening Continuum	
5. Empathic Listening	Within The Other's Frame of Reference
4. Attentive Listening	Within One's Own Frame of Reference
3. Selective Listening	
2. Pretend Listening (Patronizing)	
1. Ignoring	

Levels of Listening

At the first four levels, the listener hears with their own frame of reference in mind. But it is at Level 5 that true communication occurs. This is where the listener attempts to see things from the other person's perspective or point of view, not with their own filter/lens.

People want to be heard.
—Stephen Biller, ESQ

Level 1: Ignoring

If you have ever been ignored, there is no doubt about it. You are talking, but the other person is not giving any attention to what you are saying.

Now, it is possible the person did not hear you. If that's the case, it's not ignoring.

Level 2: Pretend Listening

To truly hear someone takes time and attention. Pretend listeners give you the impression they hear what you say, and they may hear some of your words, but they are not "present." They may nod their head or offer another gesture to indicate they are listening, but they are not giving you their full attention.

> *If you are thinking of what to say next, you are not listening.*
> —Beth Rowlett

Level 3: Selective Listening

The next level is selective listening. The person who listens selectively only wants part of the message, but not all. They are probably the person who says, "So, what's your point?" They are quick to interrupt the person who is speaking, or they have the tendency to finish the other person's sentences.

Level 4: Attentive Listening

Attentive listeners offer their time and attention. But they are one step short of being empathic listeners because attentive listeners hear from their frame of reference. They don't try to put themselves in the other person's shoes.

Listen. Really listen.

Level 5: Empathic Listening

Empathic listening is intentional. The person who develops this skill listens not only to the other person's words—they listen for what the other person means. They are willing to give their time *and* full attention to truly hear the other person.

> *To truly listen means to transcend your autobiography, to get out of your own frame of reference, out of your own value system, out of your own history and judging tendencies, and to get deeply into the frame of reference or viewpoint of another person. This is called empathic listening. It is a very, very rare skill. But it is more than a skill. Much more.*
> **—Stephen R. Covey,** *The 8th Habit*

> *Listening is a gift. It says I value you, even if we disagree.*
> **—Beth Rowlett**

Listening and Leadership

I came across this insightful study that investigates the relationship between effective listening and leadership. The author of the study, Battalion Chief Gregory L. Rynders, reached this conclusion: "The results indicate that there is a positive relationship between effective leadership and effective listening skills. Effective leaders apparently hear what others have to say and empathize with their points of view."

Become a Skilled Listener

According to Michael Lombardo and Robert Eichinger, skilled listeners model the following behaviors:
- Practices active listening
- Will hear people out
- Can accurately restate others' opinions, even when they disagree

Listening is a skill that we can sharpen continuously. (You can learn to be a whole-body listener.) In the past, I had a really tough time hearing people out, especially when I disagreed. But over the years, I have worked hard to develop my ability to listen. I am thankful for those who helped me to develop in this area. It requires work; and it is well worth the effort.

Empathic Listening

Of the levels of listening described by Stephen Covey, empathic listening is the most difficult to master but brings great dividends.

Empathy is defined as "the ability to understand and share the feelings of another." In other words, an empathic listener lets the speaker express what they think or feel.

Empathic listening requires one to be fully present, a willingness to hear the speaker's words, and a desire to truly understand the meaning of what is being communicated.

Effective Leadership

As it relates to effective leadership, the study sites five things effective leaders do that make them effective. They are:
- Communicate well
- Listen effectively
- Demonstrate approachability
- Delegate effectively
- Lead by example

Think back and reflect on the leaders to whom you have reported. If they were effective leaders, they probably possessed all of these traits (and more). Most of all, their ability to listen effectively made a positive impression on you.

Summary

This study confirms what we already know: there is a positive relationship between listening and effective leadership.

Effective leaders listen. They do not pretend to know it all because it is impossible for one person to know everything. They rely on the talented, capable individuals on their team. And they show it by asking for input from and listening to what their direct reports have to say.

SHARPEN THE SAW

"Sharpen the saw" is about renewal, the prerequisite for continuous improvement. It is Habit 7 of Stephen Covey's habits of highly effective people. It is the capstone of the three habits outlined in Private Victory and the three habits described in Public Victory.

Sharpen the saw focuses on ways to renew and develop in four areas:
- Physical
- Social/Emotional
- Mental
- Spiritual

Physical

My husband is a life and business coach for athletes. Since an athlete's physical condition is so critical to their success, he tells his clients that their health is their wealth.

Although you may not think of yourself as a professional athlete, you are a professional. Your performance is intricately tied to your ability to stay well and withstand pressure. Therefore, it is critical that you take care of yourself and maintain good health.

To sharpen your saw in this area, it is important to engage in consistent exercise, eat a healthy diet, and get adequate amounts of rest on a daily basis.

Social/Emotional

A leader brings out the best in themselves and others.

It is my natural personality to enjoy being around other people. I am energized by that. But to maintain my social and emotional health, I take measures to spend most of my time with positive people who focus on bettering themselves.

There are times when I interact with negative people or those who seem to thrive on conflict. At those times I must use effective conflict management skills, which includes minimizing my time in their "space."

This helps me use my emotional energy wisely and preserve my emotional health.

Mental

Another area to "sharpen the saw" is mentally. This includes what you take in through what you read, listen to, and even talk about. I love learning, so this is a relatively easy area for me.

One way I expand my knowledge is by reading. For example, I recently embarked on a twelve-month study of *The 8th Habit*.

When presented with the opportunity to join the study group, I was reluctant. First, a year seemed like a long time. Second, if I committed to the study that meant (for me) there was no turning back. If I signed on, I would do my level best to finish.

Well, guess what? At the time of this writing, I have completed month seven. I can hardly wait for the next five. (Smile!)

I share this to encourage you to make it a priority develop your mental capacity. When you do, you will see some very positive results. You will see growth. And growth is good.

Spiritual

Daily quality quiet time is a must for me. It is the primary way I preserve and restore my spiritual health. Mornings work best for me, giving me the opportunity to jump-start my day.

My "quiet time" usually lasts thirty minutes (or more when possible). During this time, I read and journal. It's one of the most refreshing times of my day—a key way to "sharpen my saw."

Sharpen Your Saw

Is your "saw" dull? Then it's time to sharpen your saw—physically, mentally, socially/emotionally, and spiritually. Don't hesitate. Start today.

If you have not done so already, write your goals for each of these areas. Here is a sample of my goals:

- Establish daily routines/rituals that contribute to my spiritual, mental, emotional, physical, relational and financial well-being.
- Review goals daily.
- Prioritize action items in planner when preparing for the week.
- Record accomplishments.
- Celebrate achievements!

Hopefully, this will serve as a guide to help you develop your goals.

DEALING WITH DIFFICULTY

Dealing with difficulty, be it a difficult situation or a difficult person, takes skill and will.

Skill—because you must determine what is needed to address the situation appropriately

Will—because you need the courage and motivation to take action

> *This just might be a good problem to have; solving it*
> *will develop your critical thinking skills.*

Dealing with Difficult Situations

On any given day, you will encounter many situations that need to be discussed and addressed. Some of those will be "difficult" situations.

Most often, a situation is described as difficult when it places undue demands or requires extra effort to address. I often call it an obstacle or "results I did not want" (or expect).

In other words, the situation poses a problem. And the "difficulty" stems from the lack of an apparent solution. There is an issue that is difficult to get past, and it needs to be corrected or addressed before forward progress can be realized.

At this time, taking a step back may prove helpful. Often, when we are too close to the "problem," the solution is often very difficult to see.

> *Use every adversity to stimulate you to creative survival.*
> —Eugene Peterson

Dealing with Difficult People

Some situations are labeled as difficult because of the people involved. Not only is there a problem to be solved—it is exacerbated by conflict between the parties involved in the situation.

A person may be described as "difficult" because they refuse to listen. They may be so emotional that they will not (or cannot) listen to reason. I must admit that, at times, I have been that "difficult person."

In this scenario, not only must you deal with the issue or problem at hand, you also must also use skill in human interaction to level the "communication" field.

If you and the person(s) involved cannot come to some common ground, you lose focus on the true issue that needs to be resolved. And it will impede progress.

Tips for Dealing with Difficulty

When dealing with difficult people and situations, don't forget to BREATHE!
—Coach Gwen

When you find yourself in a difficult situation, BREATHE! It's amazing how taking such a seemingly small action can deliver powerful results. Not convinced? Try it! Take time each day to breathe deeply. I recommend three times a day for ninety seconds each time. If you do this, you will see what a difference it can make. You won't know until you try it! It really is possible to use adversity to move you forward.

Learn to appreciate difficult days.
— Sarah Young

WHAT YOU EXPECT

Understanding and communicating what you expect sets the stage for success. It will help you identify goals and objectives and frame interactions with your co-workers. Understanding what you want from each party will help minimize your frustrations and theirs. It will also help you determine the standard of performance you will set for yourself and your team. Therefore, take some time to list your expectations in these four areas:
- Yourself
- Your Boss
- Your Direct Reports
- Your Peers

There are no traffic jams along the extra mile.
—Ken Evoy

What You Expect of Yourself

Whether you found your leadership position or it found you, it stands to reason that your demonstrated performance set you apart from your peers. If that is the case, you probably hold yourself to a high standard of performance, not settling for average or mediocre work. This is good! It serves as a solid foundation on which to build success in your leadership role.

Starting with your job description, determine what you must accomplish in your position. Identify how you will measure success. Lay out a plan to meet or exceed the expectations you have of yourself.

What You Expect of Your Boss

Although we may not verbalize it, we do have expectations of our boss. Based on my experience, people want a boss to be fair, respectful, and cultivate an environment that fosters teamwork.

We expect our boss to communicate their expectations and give feedback about how well we are performing against objectives. Although we will receive constructive criticism, we seek to receive some positive feedback.

We also expect a boss to help us use our skills and talents to the best of our ability and provide opportunities for growth.

Now, we all have different needs. So, you must be specific about your expectations, evaluate if they are reasonable, and determine the best way to engage in two-way communication with your boss.

Discussing this with your boss may be uncomfortable and even seem daunting, but developing your communication skills related to this area can be beneficial in the long term.

What You Expect of Your Direct Reports

The same holds true with your direct reports. Be up front about what you look for in their performance and the way you envision the team working together to reach mutual goals.

Be objective. Seek to minimize subjectivity and base those expectations on a current position/job description.

Setting goals and objectives aligned with the organization's strategic objectives, monitoring progress and giving feedback on performance are key aspects of your role.

It's important to develop a strategy to tap into the minds of your direct reports to discover what they expect from you, their leader.

As a leader, you have certain expectations of your direct reports individually and collectively as a team. Usually though, we seldom think about taking the time to find out what our team expects of us. We assume we already know. Or we may not really care what they expect.

But leaders who lead not only care about what their direct reports expect; they take the time to find out. The best way to do that is by talking with their direct reports.

In each of my roles, I made it a point to talk with my direct reports as a group. As soon as possible, make it a point to meet with your team. If they do not know you, this is an opportunity to introduce yourself and meet each person on the team. If they do know you (and you have worked with them before), this is an opportunity to become visible as a leader of the group.

During this meeting, you can set the stage for building rapport and communicate your intentions of meeting with each team member.

Since teams are made up of individuals, it is important to meet with each direct report to find out what they expect of you as their leader. This may seem foreign and unnecessary. But my greatest success has come when I took the time to talk with my direct reports. More importantly, I took the time to let them talk to me.

By following the discovery process, I was able to identify what each team member expected. I was also able to gauge what was important to each member. Armed with this information, I could also help manage their expectations. Many leaders resist finding out what their team expects. Why? Because they believe it takes too much time. And they are pressed for time.

The truth is this: If you do not have the time to do it right the first time, you do not have the time to do it over. Therefore, take the time now; make it a priority. Finding out what your team expects will save you time in the long run.

Business success requires that managers find a means of tapping into the highest potential of all their employees.
—Dr. R. Roosevelt Thomas Jr.

Time must be maximized, not trivialized. We should take advantage of it because we can never get it back.
—Dr. Tony Evans

What You Expect of Your Peers

Although you do not have direct authority over your peers or their performance, you do have a level of influence. Clearly communicating what you bring to the team can lay a good foundation for working well together.

Finding out what your peers expect is important for at least two reasons:
- It fosters two-way communication.
- It fosters trust.

Both are critical for working well together. You also get the opportunity to discuss the expectations you have of your peers. So, it really is a two-way street.

Who Is My Peer?

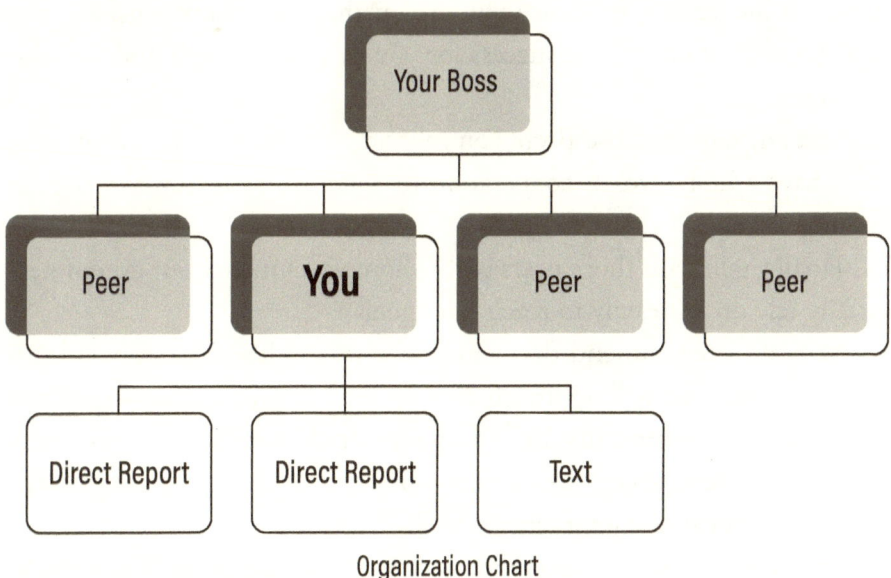

Organization Chart

In most organizations, your peer is anyone who meets one of the following:
- You report to the same boss.

- You do not report to the same boss, but you work together on a consistent basis to achieve common goals.

(Note: Your peer does not have to be a member of your department/functional group.)

> *Trust [is] the glue of relationships.*
> —Stephen R. Covey

What Your Peers Expect

Where Do I Start?

First, start with what I call "Near Peers." These are co-workers who report to the same boss. Since you are on the same team, working well together will be critical for success for you as a department and for your function.

Second, talk to those peers you rely on heavily and with whom you must have a high level of cooperation to reach your organizational goals and objectives.

Finally, talk with those peers with whom you interact but do not necessarily rely on as heavily to reach your goals.

Why do I recommend that you follow this order? Because you must prioritize how you will approach this process. Doing so this way allows you to start at the most urgent and important. Also, this process will help you build working relationships that contribute to success not only in the short term, but in the long term as well.

To record what your peers expect, use Expectation at Work worksheet located in the appendix.

LEADERSHIP QUOTES FOR ACHIEVERS

The quotes in this section are designed to inspire you to reach increasing levels of success. You have the potential to be and do great things, to positively impact the world where you are. A quote, well said, can be like a "vitamin": good to you and good for you. Keep your favorite quotes handy to remind yourself that you are an achiever.

Achievement Quotes

"More gold has been mined from the thoughts of men than has been taken from the earth."
—Napoleon Hill

"You have not found your place until all your faculties are roused, and your whole nature consents and approves of the work you are doing."
—Orison Swett Marden

"Prosperity belongs to those who learn new things the fastest."
—Paul Zane Pilzer

"Success is not only the financial wealth you accumulate, it is also about being a leader, improving your relationships, living healthfully, and making a real difference in the world."
—Darren Hardy

"Big results require big ambitions."
—Heraclitus

"It takes less work to succeed than fail."
—W. Clement Stone

"Wherever you see a successful business,
someone once made a courageous decision."
—Peter F. Drucker

"Trust and reputation are not discretionary. They are as necessary
in business as the people in whom they reside."
—Tony Alessandra

"A leader is one who knows the way, goes the way, and shows the way."
—John C. Maxwell

Relationship Quotes

"The most powerful and predictable people-builders
are praise and encouragement."
—Brian Tracy

"The best executive is the one who has sense enough to pick good people
to do what he wants done, and self-restraint to keep from meddling
with them while they do it."
—Theodore Roosevelt

"If you find it in your heart to care for somebody else, you will have succeeded."
—Maya Angelou

"The most important single ingredient in the formula for success is knowing how to get along with people."
—**Theodore Roosevelt**

"You must look into people, as well as at them."
—**Lord Chesterfield**

"You can make more friends in two months by becoming interested in other people than you can in two years by trying to get other people interested in you."
—**Dale Carnegie**

Inspirational Quotes

"If it is true that for everything there is a season, I believe this is ours."
—**Denise Bissonette**[9]

Attitude

Everything can be taken from a man but one thing: to choose one's attitude in any given set of circumstances, to choose one's own way."
—**Victor E. Frankel**

"What lies beyond us and what lies before us are tiny matters when compared to what lies within us."
—**Ralph Waldo Emerson**

"Some people are always grumbling because roses have thorns. I am thankful that thorns have roses."
—**Alphonse Karr**

"We spend far too much time on the ground, unaware of the heights to which we can soar. Perhaps it's not what we are that holds us back, but what we think we aren't!"
—Denise Bissonette

"Heroism consists of hanging on one minute longer."
—Anonymous

"Expect to find abundance and do not be discouraged or slowed by evidence to the contrary."
—Denise Bissonnette

"What lies beyond us and what lies before is are tiny matters when compared to what lies within us."
—Ralph Waldo Emerson

Opportunity

"We have tremendous power to control our destinies. We each have everything it takes to change our world."
—Denise Bissonnette

"Opportunities come from knocking on doors until they open."
—An Opportunist

"Procrastination is opportunity's natural assassin."
—Anonymous

"Some men go through a forest and see no firewood."
—English Proverb

"As is your sort of mind, so is your sort of search; you'll find what you desire."
—Robert Browning

"Learning to ask new questions is the beginning of creating new opportunity."
—Denise Bissonnette

"Make no small plans for they have no power to stir the soul."
—Anonymous

Goals

"We know that if a goal is to be achieved, it must be embraced by the person him/herself."
—Denise Bissonnette

"We can never exceed our own expectations."
—Lao-Tzu

"Many people adopt modest goals in an attempt to avoid disappointment. Unfortunately, low aspirations tend to be self-fulfilling."
—Anonymous

Change

"As we have learned from futile attempts to break down walls of resistance, the gates of change only open from the inside."
—Denise Bissonnette

"A different world cannot be built by indifferent people."
—Anonymous

"When one senses that everything to be reaped from a particular endeavor has been reaped, it is time to move on to more fertile ground."
—Denise Bissonnette

> "The difficulty lies not so much in developing new ideas
> as in escaping from old ones."
> —John Maynard Keynes

> "The road to success is always under construction."
> —Anonymous

> "Genuine beginnings begin within us, even when they are brought
> to our attention by external opportunities."
> —William Bridges

Leading Change, Leading Transformation

These quotes are excerpts from John Kotter's book *Leading Change*. His book is one of my favorites. He is an expert in helping us understand strategies for navigating change and transition.

> "Change requires skill and will."

> "Useful change ... is never employed effectively unless it is driven by high–quality leadership, not just excellent management."

> "Successful transformation is 70 to 90 percent leadership and only 10 to 30 percent management."

> "Only leadership can motivate the actions needed to alter behavior in any significant way."

> "Leadership is the engine that drives change."

> "The rate of change is not going to slow down anytime soon. If anything, competition in most industries will probably speed up even more in the next few decades."

"For change efforts to be successful, behaviors must be altered. If behavior isn't altered, we're doomed to repeat past mistakes."

"Everyone has a stake in orchestrating change in their organization."

"Transformations always fail to achieve their objectives when complacency levels are high."

"Real transformations take time."

"Change sticks only when it becomes 'the way we do things around here,' when it seeps into the very bloodstream of the work unit or corporate body."

"The problem for us today is that stability is no longer the norm."

"The combination of cultures that resist change and managers who have not been taught how to create change is lethal."

"Transformation requires sacrifice, dedication, and creativity, none of which usually comes with coercion."

"If change were easy, you wouldn't need all that effort."

"Don't underestimate how hard it is to drive people out of their comfort zones."

"Without a sense of urgency, people won't give that extra effort that is often essential.

"Without credible communication, and a lot of it, employees' hearts and minds are never captured."

Nothing undermines change more than behavior by important individuals that is inconsistent with the verbal communication."

"Without short-term wins, too many employees give up or actively join the resistance."

A free ebook edition is available with the purchase of this book.

To claim your free ebook edition:
1. Visit MorganJamesBOGO.com
2. Sign your name CLEARLY in the space
3. Complete the form and submit a photo of the entire copyright page
4. You or your friend can download the ebook to your preferred device

A **FREE** ebook edition is available for you or a friend with the purchase of this print book.

CLEARLY SIGN YOUR NAME ABOVE

Instructions to claim your free ebook edition:
1. Visit MorganJamesBOGO.com
2. Sign your name CLEARLY in the space above
3. Complete the form and submit a photo of this entire page
4. You or your friend can download the ebook to your preferred device

Print & Digital Together Forever.

Snap a photo   Free ebook   Read anywhere

www.ingramcontent.com/pod-product-compliance
Lightning Source LLC
Chambersburg PA
CBHW020859180526
45163CB00007B/2559